YOUR UNDERGRA

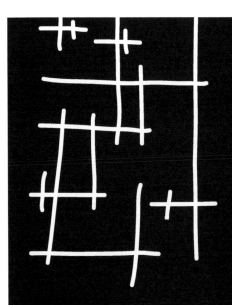

MARK FORSHAW
YOUR UNDERGRADUATE
PSYCHOLOGY
PROJECT
A BPS GUIDE

BPS Blackwell

© 2004 by Mark Forshaw
A BPS Blackwell book

BLACKWELL PUBLISHING
350 Main Street, Malden, MA 02148-5020, USA
9600 Garsington Road, Oxford OX4 2DQ, UK
550 Swanston Street, Carlton, Victoria 3053, Australia

First published 2004 by The British Psychological Society and Blackwell Publishing Ltd

3   2006

Library of Congress Cataloging-in-Publication Data

Forshaw, Mark.
  Your undergraduate psychology project : a BPS guide / Mark Forshaw.—1st ed.
    p. cm.
  "A BPS Blackwell book."
  Includes bibliographical references and index.
  ISBN 1-4051-1937-3 (hbk : alk. paper)—ISBN 1-4051-1936-5 (pbk. : alk. paper)
  1. Psychology—Research—Textbooks. I. Title.

BF76.5. F68 2004
150'. 72—dc22

                                                                    2004013765

ISBN-13: 978-1-4051-1937-5 (hbk : alk. paper)—ISBN-13: 978-1-4051-1936-8 (pbk. : alk.
paper)

A catalogue record for this title is available from the British Library.

Set in 10 on 12.5pt Rotis Serif
by Kolam Information Services Pvt. Ltd, Pondicherry, India

For further information on
Blackwell Publishing, visit our website:
www.blackwellpublishing.com

CONTENTS

PREFACE

This book is intended primarily for undergraduate psychology students conducting research, especially those undertaking their final-year project. It is not a book on research methods or statistics, since there are many excellent books of that type. This book provides mostly practical advice. It is divided into three sections which cover the research process. All research must first be planned, then it must be conducted, and then a report of that research is written. The structure of this book mirrors this.

You will have a supervisor or tutor assigned to help you with your research. This book is like a second supervisor. Listen to your tutor, and take all of their advice. They come first. However, they can't tell you everything, and they can't be with you at 2 a.m. as you are huddled over a computer frantically typing up a research report to be handed in the next day. This book never sleeps, of course.

This book has been like a qualitative research project for me. I have written it based upon my own experiences of being a student, as an undergraduate and as a postgraduate. I have used my understanding of the process of research from supervising hundreds of research projects at all sorts of levels, from first-year undergraduate through to PhD level. I wrote a proposal for writing this book, and this was commented on by a number of academics and a team of people at BPS Blackwell. I have given drafts of this book to academics and to students, and they have provided feedback to help shape the version you see before you. I hope that it does not end here. I welcome feedback from readers, so that any future editions can be revised and expanded. Like any research, this book could grow and get better. Please help to make this happen by writing to me, via my publishers.

Mark Forshaw, August 2004

ACKNOWLEDGEMENTS

This book has been commented on, in draft form, by the lecturers Dr David Giles and Dr Paul Castle, and the students Stephanie Roden, Joyce Tinker and Hayley Tizard. I thank them warmly for their time and their helpful suggestions. They worked at short notice, which makes their efforts all the more appreciable.

I would also like to express my gratitude to the mostly anonymous project co-ordinators in various universities around the UK who provided valuable information in response to my questionnaire which formed part of the research for this book.

My editors at BPS Blackwell, Sarah Bird and Will Maddox, have been as supportive, encouraging and good-humoured as any editors could ever be, and I am indebted to them. Most of all, they conveyed a very genuine sense that they believed in this book, which is just what an author needs.

Finally, my love to Amanda Crowfoot. There is a part of her in everything I have written, because there is a part of her in me.

PLANNING RESEARCH

You are reading this, which means that you have actually started your planning. Of course, you are probably *very* early in the process, but that doesn't matter. As some Chinese people say, a few drops of water are the start of a river. You might think that you are bad at planning things, just like some people think that they are bad at statistics or hopeless at football, but planning is something for which you don't require much natural talent (unlike the other two, perhaps). If you take a structured approach, and discipline yourself, there is no reason why you can't plan a great research project and see it right through to the end.

Research always requires good planning. You can't expect to make a good job of something so important as a research project unless you have worked out the details before you start. You need a map of the process, so to speak. You need to know what you are going to do, how you are going to set about it, what you will need to do it with, when you are going to do it, how long it will take, what is likely to go wrong, what you will do if it goes wrong and who you will need to ask for help at various points on the way. Final-year projects are usually heavily weighted in calculating a student's degree classification, and so if you want to achieve the very best degree you can you should take your research very seriously. It's normally the single most important thing you will do in a psychology course, and deserves to be well planned. In this section, advice is given on all aspects of planning, from deciding what to research through to keeping an eye on the ethical concerns to which all researchers must be sensitive.

♯ CHOOSING A RESEARCH TOPIC

Psychology departments differ in the extent to which students are expected or allowed to choose their topic of research. In some departments, lecturers suggest pieces of research and students can choose from these. In others, students are given completely free rein to select what they want to research: the lecturer's job is only to advise on this, or to troubleshoot. Therefore, this particular section is only of direct use to those students (the majority of those in the UK) who have some kind of choice to make as to what research to engage in.

If you really don't know what to research, all is not lost. Waiting for an idea to pop into your head while you walk around the supermarket or take a shower is not recommended. If the ideas aren't forthcoming, anxiety is likely to set in. If you're worrying about what to do for your project, the chances are that your anxiety will block off some of your best thoughts. We've all experienced the feeling of being too busy worrying about something to actually get on with it. Rather than fret, do something productive that could help to generate ideas. Some idea-generating methods which work for most people are given here. They've helped many of my own students in the past. Try them.

The Textbook Method

This is a method of elimination, particularly useful when you have absolutely no idea what to research. Pick a general psychology textbook, the sort of book you might use in the early stages of your studies in psychology, with chapters on just about every area of the discipline. Look at the contents list at the front, and choose from that the areas of psychology which really do interest you. That should leave you with a few chapters of the book which you then need to look into more deeply. Read those chapters, flicking through and eliminating which sub-areas you are still not interested in. Eventually you should be left with a small list of the topics which you could conceivably do some work around. After all, you chose to study psychology, and so there ought to be some aspects of it which fascinate you! Once you have done this, try to rank the topics in order of interest to you. Take your number one topic, and read the whole section of the book which is relevant to that. Take care to read in detail about the research which has already been done in this area. At this point, some ideas should start to spring to mind. Think about ways in which you could adapt previous research. Try doing a literature search using an electronic database, and reading the most recent research in your selected area. Pay attention to the Discussion sections of the articles you are reading. Here you will actually find suggestions as to further research. Why not consider taking up the gauntlet and pursuing one of these suggestions? You will impress your supervisor with your reading, and you'll be doing something which, in theory, could actually be publishable in itself. So, a few days work has led you from a complete blank through to an idea for a project at the cutting edge of psychology. Not bad, eh?

The Television Method

It's rare for a student never to watch television. Sometimes you might feel guilty because you're sitting in front of your favourite soap rather than getting on with your work. This method helps to appease your guilt, because watching television is a form of research.

All you need is a notepad and pen to accompany you while you watch. The difficult bit comes with the fact that you have to think about what you are watching. Television is full of ideas for research. If you watch programmes which feature debate, especially of *The Jerry Springer Show,* or *Trisha* type, you have a great source of material. Here you have everyday people arguing over everyday things. Ask yourself how and why. Sometimes the debate is around something quite unusual, like a non-standard family arrangement where a woman lives with two men rather than the usual one. Again, our attitudes to this kind of thing are probably worth studying.

Watch the news. Stories break all the time which can be made into psychological research. Most of the stories are directly about people. Some psychological research has been directed at studying the nature and persuasiveness of the news message in the light of the language used, the credibility of the speaker, and so on.

Watch advertisements. Why are the advertisers presenting the product in the way that they are? Is there anything unusual about the method being used? To which types of people might the advertising campaign appeal?

Watch children's programmes. If you are interested in developmental psychology, you will find a thousand ideas waiting for you. You can investigate parents' and children's opinions of various programmes, or their educational value, for example. You can look into how children's personalities may dictate their viewing preferences.

Watch comedy programmes. Good comedy relies upon a great many facets which you might like to explore. Timing is just one of them: one can easily conceive of a neat experiment where the length of time before the punch line of a joke or witty comment is delivered could actually be manipulated systematically. Imagine being able to generate a graph to show the optimal pause before making a funny comment or finishing a joke!

Watch documentaries. Some documentaries are directly relevant to psychology, some less so, but you can always find ideas there. Even ones about history or wildlife can lead to some useful research. For example, very little psychological research has been conducted into the different ways in which people view the past. Have you ever wondered why so many people have a feeling that the world before about 1950 was black-and-white? Of course, it's probably because the film footage we see from back then happens to be monochrome, but there's probably a lot to explore in those kinds of notions. Furthermore, many TV documentaries have a website where you can follow up the issues, and possibly access much more information on the issues covered in the programme.

The Pub Chat or Coffee Bar Method

You have probably guessed what this is all about. Make use of times when you hang about with friends, just chatting, whether in a bar or elsewhere. A common theme in conversation is the asking of psychological questions. Listen to people chatting. It won't be long before you hear questions like these:

- Why do people do that?
- Does anyone actually think like that?
- How does that card trick work?
- Who do you reckon wants to buy that?
- Are teen bands really promoting sexuality in young people?
- Can a leopard really change its spots?
- What makes someone want to climb a mountain?

Many of the themes which enter common conversation are worth exploring in a psychological research context. Even the dynamics of chat itself are interesting. Who talks to whom? Why? When? Not only are these things worth looking into; you'll find that other psychologists have also addressed many of these issues, so you won't be without a theoretical precedent on which to base your research.

The Internet Method

The internet is a strange place, but is replete with potential ideas for research. You can find out about people with unusual interests. You can access forums and bulletin boards where people discuss various issues, and you can even find lists of ideas for research, especially by seeking out the websites of academics and looking at the kinds of research they are engaged in and are often hoping to conduct in the future. Many search engines actually feature a random site button, where you will be directed to somewhere without knowing where it will be. Sometimes, you can find some fascinating things in this way.

Think Again!

Although departments do differ a little in respect to ethical procedures, you should be aware that certain project ideas are usually non-starters. There is no point wasting time researching an idea only to be told that there is no way that you will be permitted to investigate that particular area of psychology.

Generally, you will not be allowed to work directly with prison inmates or ex-prisoners, especially those with a history of violent crime, paedophilia, or other sexual crime. You will not usually be permitted to access people who are mentally ill, especially those with schizophrenia or other illnesses which involve significant disorders of the thought processes. You will not be able to conduct studies which involve administering electric shock or pain, however mild. (Pain studies are *sometimes* allowable, and your supervisor will advise.) You will not be permitted to do any research involving showing people hard-core pornography, or scenes of extreme violence, including images of real death and injury. You will not be able to conduct studies on the psychophysiology of sexual arousal, using equipment such as the penile plethysmograph. There are probably many more examples, but this list covers the main things you should steer well clear of.

♯ SELF-INTEREST

Often students approach me with an idea for research which comes from their own experience or personal interests. This can be a great source of inspiration. For example, you might be a skateboarding expert who wants to investigate the formation of social identities surrounding the skateboarding community, or a chess player who would like to test the working memories of other chess players. If a particular issue fascinates you, you are motivated to do a great job of the research.

There are, however, some issues you should consider when pursuing a research topic stemming from a personal desire to understand some phenomenon.

- Will researching the issue bring up terrible memories or encourage a poor mood, which might affect your motivation? This could happen when you research something such as bullying, if you have been bullied yourself.
- Will your personal experiences influence the nature of your research and force you into following through only those ideas you agree with, thus meaning that you miss out on some new ideas which do not fit your own experiences?
- Will you run up against ethical problems, for example, where you wish to research anorexia nervosa because you were once affected by it or still are? What I mean by this is that some people might argue that your own history might affect the research in some way that could be negative. A person with experience of anorexia nervosa interviewing someone else might actually become a role model for that person, for example. After all, as many qualitative researchers argue, the interviewer is sometimes in a subtle position of power and influence. It might not be very likely, but it is possible, and in considering the ethical dimensions of research we must reflect on the unlikely as well as the likely consequences.

If your honest answers to any of these questions might be 'yes', then you would be well advised to think of another topic to pursue. Denscombe (2002, p. 35) sums this up as follows:

> It is crucial to distinguish between the positive and healthy influence of having a personal interest in a topic which will operate to sustain the researcher through hard times, and the detrimental impact of having such a commitment and passion for a topic that the researcher approaches the area with conclusions already set in his or her mind and an unwillingness to discover what is not desired.

If you intend to conduct qualitative research, you must be ready and willing to admit to your own personal preconceptions and experiences when you write up the research, since this is an essential part of the process of explaining to the reader the way in which you have come to your conclusions. If your experiences are necessarily private, you should think twice before taking the first steps down such a path.

REPLICATION VERSUS NOVELTY

Replicating a study, i.e. looking to see if you can achieve the same result as someone else by copying their method and analysis in detail, is something which rarely gets done these days. One reason for this is that there is a great pressure on academics to publish, and a great pressure on journals to publish only new and exciting studies, since space on the printed page is at a premium. Therefore, when the editor of a journal is faced with a choice between publishing a replication or publishing a brand-new study, they often tend to choose the latter. What has happened, therefore, is that replications have become seen as 'second-class' studies. There is a danger in this, because without replications we can be less confident in the research we have conducted and on which we have based our theories. However, partly because of the apparent unpopularity of replications at the highest level, students are sometimes also discouraged from conducting replications as the research in their final-year project. Another reason is that replications can be done without any creativity or ingenuity.

If your department prefers you not to conduct a replication, then of course you must honour this, but you might find that you can compromise and carry out research in two parts. A neat and worthwhile project can result from conducting a replication of previous research *followed by* a further development of the original experiment, thus carrying knowledge onwards. This approach can be very useful, especially to a student who is unsure about what topic to research. The topic simply presents itself, and it is often easier to develop previous research than invent a new strand of it.

One way in which replication can be particularly valuable is in testing out cultural or historical factors. For example, some early studies of the influences of advertising and the media were carried out decades ago, when television was much less commonplace. Today, people are generally considered to be more media-aware, and possibly even cynical about advertising. Therefore, looking at how the trends observed in the 1950s and 1960s might have changed could prove fruitful.

Genuinely novel research, of course, presents its own problems. Remember that if you have a great idea for new research it ought to be grounded in some kind of practical problem which requires an answer, or it should be aimed at adding to existing theory in some way. 'Wacky' or eccentric research is not typically encouraged unless it also has a serious aspect to it.

⊞ PURE VERSUS APPLIED RESEARCH

Another important characteristic of research hinges around the pure/applied distinction. It is fair to say that, for psychology academics, the days of pure research are almost gone, and this has started to affect student research as well. Research needs to be funded, and with very limited money available the work that tends to attract funds is that which has a clear application to some area of life. Finding things out 'for the sake of it' has become a minority activity, with most attention being paid to directing research at answering questions which seem to actually *need* answering. Therefore, in order to train you for this world, your lecturers are likely to want you to choose a research topic with an obvious purpose. If you cannot think of a good reason why you ought to carry out research of the kind you are proposing, you should perhaps reconsider.

There is also an ethical dimension to pure and applied research. Not only is applied research all about making best use of resources, it tends to avoid some of the dubious aspects of research, which in the past has included controversial topics such as racial differences in abilities. If you decide that you want to know if different kinds of people differ in some way, you must ask yourself two questions. First, why do you want to know it? Second, what could become of the findings of your research? You have a responsibility not to create information which can be misused, or misinterpreted, or reinterpreted for an unethical purpose. There is a political aspect to all our lives, including the research that we do, and applied research is often safer because it is directed at a particular problem and is generally aimed at doing good and making the world a better place.

♯ RESEARCHING THE PROJECT: FINDING LITERATURE

Finding literature relevant to a project can be very easy or very difficult, depending upon how you go about it and what it is that you are trying to find. The first point of call is often your supervisor. If you are researching something within their field of expertise, you will often find that they can suggest the sorts of things which you need to go away and read, perhaps even giving you the names of key researchers in the area. Of course, you must not rely solely on your supervisor. Most of the work has to be done by you, and that means systematically searching through electronic databases to identify appropriate articles.

Using Internet Search Engines

Generally, my advice on using internet search engines would be this: don't. Internet search engines are not academic databases. Someone once said that 90 per cent of everything is junk. This may or may not be true, but there is an awful lot of junk on the internet. If you try finding relevant literature using the internet, you will have to filter out that rubbish and you might sometimes not know the difference between information and nonsense because some of the nonsense on the internet is masquerading as information. This sounds harsh, but it is sadly the case. There is a good reason why we have journals, and a good reason why we have electronic databases which enable us to search the content of the journals for specific themes. The reason is that articles in journals are subject to what is called peer-review. When someone submits an article to a journal, the editor first decides if it is relevant to that journal. If so, it is usually sent to two or three experts in the field to comment on it. Only the articles which are highly rated by the reviewers are likely to be published. Therefore, there are considerable 'quality-control' checks on the nature of the information contained in journals. The internet isn't like that. If I want to post a picture of my dog wearing a dress, I can put it on the internet and no one questions it. Similarly, I could probably conduct some bad research, apply the wrong statistical tests to the data, write it up in terrible English, and then post it somewhere on the internet where it *looks* like it might be some proper academic work.

Most of the electronic databases that you should use for finding appropriate literature are internet-based, but that's almost all you should really use the internet for when looking for articles. Never do a search in a standard search engine and expect to find anything of high academic quality. If you do this, you'll end up looking for a single needle in millions of haystacks.

Snowballing and Searching via Citations

Snowballing refers to a method of widening a literature search based upon the literature already read. In order to have an idea in the first place, you might have come across an article or two which spurred your interest. This can be your starting point. Look at the reference lists of the papers you have in front of you, and you will find many other articles mentioned which you could then check up on. This process could carry on and on, of course, but after a while you will start to come across the same articles again and again in reference lists, at which point you will probably be approaching the point when you are exhausting the relevant literature. This can be a very slow process, but it is quite a systematic one, since you are using other people's literature searching to shape your own.

A second, similar method is to identify a few key authors in the area you are researching and then look them up in a citation catalogue, such as the

A GOOD RESEARCHER IS
OFTEN FOUND IMMERSED
IN THE LITERATURE

Social Sciences Citation Index, which your library will probably have access to either in printed form or electronically. You can look for a key author, and you will find a list of all of the other authors who have referred to their work, thus allowing you to identify who the *other* important authors are.

Using Electronic Databases

Your library will have access to a range of electronic databases, and some of these are specific to psychology (such as *PsychINFO*). It is not appropriate to give you advice on using all of these here, since your library will have details of them and usually your librarian will show you how to access them and use them if you ask. However, it is important to give you some information regarding the use of such databases, since they will become your electronic friends during the course of your project (even though at times you might feel like they are in league with the enemy). In addition to *PsychINFO*, which deals with psychological literature, you might also find yourself using *ERIC* (a database of educational literature), and a medical database such as *MEDLINE*. If you are conducting a project in health psychology, you might also like to look at the *British Medical Journal* online at *www.bmj.com*.

Such databases are only useful when you know how to use them properly. You need to be aware that you cannot type in the title of your project and expect to find literature based upon that! The more you can identify key words related to your research, the more you can find relevant articles. Part of the problem can be the fact that, as a psychologist in training, you don't always know the key words you should use. One way around this is to find just one relevant article and then look at the key words associated with it. Then you can direct your search using those, letting the authors do the work for you.

Boolean Operators

Most internet search engines and those attached to particular databases allow you to fine-tune a search by the use of a particular set of terms which are well known to mathematicians and logicians: Boolean operators (named after George Boole). The main three you might use are AND, NOT and OR, usually typed this way, in capitals. If you type 'fish OR chips' you will pick up everything with the word 'fish' in it, and everything with the word 'chips'. If you type 'fish AND chips' you will pick up everything which contains both of the words (but not necessarily in the same place in a sentence). 'Fish NOT chips' will only select items which contain 'fish' but definitely do not mention 'chips'. Finally, if you want the actual phrase 'fish and chips', you need to type it in quotation marks thus: "fish and chips". Boolean terms can be very useful when you are searching for a particular author. You might want everything by Hans Eysenck, but nothing by Michael Eysenck or Sybil Eysenck.

You can often use brackets to hone in on a very particular thing. Consider this search term:

    (fish OR chips) AND (salt NOT vinegar)

What do you think this will find? Compare this to:

(fish AND chips) NOT (salt OR vinegar)

Consider moving the brackets around a bit, and you will change things again.

In addition to Boolean operators, you can also normally use 'wildcards' to help your search. A wildcard allows you to say that you want to search for anything containing a particular string of letters or numbers. The standard wildcard symbol is *. You might want to search for a 'family' of words which all come from a single stem. For example, you might want to find all articles pertaining to the concept of 'attitudes'. By typing in only 'attitudes', you could miss out anything which does not feature that particular word but does feature the word 'attitude', and the word 'attitudinal'. If you type in 'attitud*' you will catch them all. Similarly, 'psycholog*' will pick up 'psychology', 'psychological', 'psychologically' and even 'psychologies'. 'Crim*' picks up 'crime', 'criminal', 'criminally', 'criminology', 'criminological', and so on.

Narrowing Searches

When searching through databases for relevant literature, there are two situations which tend to make people groan. The first is when there seems to be nothing written on a subject whatsoever. The second is where 38,906 articles contain the keywords you typed in. That is, where there is simply too much literature to absorb. In these cases, some of these articles will actually be irrelevant, but you don't know what until you start to check them out. Of course, no one would expect you to read the abstracts of tens of thousands of articles for an undergraduate research project! You need some way of making the task more manageable. Using Boolean search terms like those mentioned above will help, but there are also a few more things you can do. Try to limit your search to articles published in English, unless, of course, you will have no problem reading Japanese or Russian journals! Most databases will allow you to select only those articles in the English language. This will normally only cut down the search results by around five per cent, but that's still five in every hundred you won't have to read through. Another possibility to reduce your workload is to exclude older articles. While sometimes you might miss some extremely important material this way, you ought to generally focus on more recent work in any current research report. By selecting nothing older than around five years, you will often cut away around a half of the listed articles. If you are worried about making sure that you catch all of the important older literature, don't. When you start reading some of your chosen articles, you will find that some of them refer to the older pieces of work anyway, and so you can then chase these references up separately in a manual, rather than electronic, fashion.

Storing Search Results

Databases of literature usually allow you to email the results of your searches to yourself. I strongly recommend that you do this, and then check that the email has arrived before you log off. You can normally select how much information you want to be sent to you. You should think carefully about this before you email the results to yourself, because the 'full record', as it is called, contains a lot of information that you probably don't need. You can specify which fields you require, and most of the time you would only need a few fields like AUTHOR, YEAR, TITLE, SOURCE and ABSTRACT. By reducing the size of each record in a search that you send to yourself, you will reduce the file transfer time via email, make it more likely that you can save the searches on a floppy disk, save paper in printing off those records, and cut down on the time taken to fish through them for the crucial detail.

How Many References?

A common question that students ask is 'How many references should I have in my report?', and this is often followed up with 'How many should be journal articles and how many can be books?' Most supervisors answer this question with a statement like 'It depends...' or by asking the student how long a piece of string is. I'm afraid that there is no straight answer to this kind of student query. Every piece of research is different, and the background literature to some areas of research is enormous, whereas for other topics it is almost nonexistent. Of course, that doesn't help you, as a student. Therefore, here is a vague and non-committal answer to the age-old question.

Aim to cite journal articles more than books, since journals are where you find original reports of research, and journals are peer-reviewed, which means that various checks and balances have been made to control the quality of the research reported therein. As for the ratio of one to the other, it is probably safe to say that an excellent research report often makes no mention of books, and is generally based almost exclusively on research papers. You should be aware, though, that some books are what we call 'scholarly', which means that they are collections of research papers, conference proceedings, and so on, and these are generally acceptable to refer to.

Now for an even more difficult issue. If you are walking a well-trodden path, where there is a lot of relevant literature, you should aim to summarise a good portion of it. This does not mean that your References section should contain thousands of items. In fact, many journal editors request that writers keep their References section as short as is realistically possible. When you are working on something that is very new, this should be quite easy anyway. Generally, stick to referring to only those articles which are directly relevant. For the average undergraduate student project, in my experience, any fewer than 10 references is normally frowned upon. Somewhere between 10 and 20 is starting to look respectable, and around 20 to 30 tends to 'look good'. If you have more than 30, you *might* be over-egging the pudding. However, do consult your supervisor on this issue, because this is a very broad generalisation.

Statistics on the Internet

There are a number of places on the internet where you can access some useful information that you might want to use in researching a project and writing a literature review or introduction. For example, you will find official statistics at *www.statistics.gov.uk*, the site of the Office for National Statistics in the UK. If you want to know things like the number of births per year, or deaths, or marriages, or how many people have multiple sclerosis, you should look here first. Most countries in the Western world have similar sites which will then allow you to make comparisons across nationalities or cultures.

⊞ CHOOSING A METHOD

There are two main ways of selecting a method. The first is choosing a method which you are comfortable using, and ignoring the rest. This is not to be recommended, since a good psychologist ought to be able to use whatever method is the best to investigate the issue in question. However, we need to be realistic, too. If you really don't understand mixed designs (or the split-plot ANOVA you'll be using to analyse the results), or if you can't get your head around grounded theory or discourse analysis, then you probably won't achieve particularly good marks if you try to use them in your project. Therefore, using a method (and subsequent analysis) which you truly understand is sensible.

The second, and preferable, approach is to choose the most appropriate method for what you want to research. Knowing what the best method is involves a degree of skill which develops over time, and your supervisor will be able to help with this. Everyone has their favourite methods, however, and you should make sure that your supervisor is actually able to offer the right research methods expertise to help you with your project. Don't just assume that every lecturer is capable of conducting every type of research, or even interested in doing so. Coming to a decision as to an appropriate method to employ is a matter of negotiation between you and your supervisor.

Single-Case Designs

Single-case designs tend to be rare in student projects, although there is no obvious reason why. Working on a piece of research involving just one participant does not mean that the research is necessarily any easier than research conducted with hundreds of participants. A lot depends upon the nature of the research.

Single-case designs are mainly experimental in nature, although not usually subject to statistical analysis. In some ways, they are more difficult to conduct than studies involving large numbers of participants, since a single individual is often very sensitive to small fluctuations and discrepancies in the research which would be diluted in studies with groups of individuals.

If you really want to conduct a single-case study but your supervisor is not convinced that this is a good idea, perhaps because they favour studies with more participants, a compromise is to suggest a single-case-series design. This is where a number of separate single-case designs are conducted, each in the same way, and the trends in the data examined by representing each person as one line on the graph.

Bear in mind that the amount of work involved in the simplest single-case design, such as A-B-A, is probably not appropriate for a final-year research project conducted over nine months or so. Therefore, you should aim for a more elaborate design, such as A-B-A-B-A, or involving multiple 'treatments', such as A-B-A-B-A-C-A-C-A.

Case Studies

Case studies are often mistaken for single-case designs. However, they are not the same thing. To an extent, the case study is the qualitative version of a single-case design. Instead of looking at individuals and measuring things with numbers, the case study deals mainly with words, and the diary method is a common tool for conducting case studies. Again, these are not commonly conducted in student projects, because case studies are most often used in clinical, forensic, educational and psychotherapeutic contexts, and students do not generally provide therapy for people, and are, by definition, not trained clinical, forensic or educational psychologists with access to clients.

Therefore, if you like the case study method, you must think very carefully about what you are aiming to find out and from whom. You are only likely to be able to work with a participant who is not a patient or client in some professional context, and so this cuts down on what you might look at. One perfectly acceptable case study could be to use a qualitative method to plough through a diary kept by a person giving up smoking or chocolate, for example. This might provide some useful insights for health psychology which most studies to date might have failed to uncover.

Choosing Qualitative Methods

Qualitative and quantitative methods are not always opposed to each other. While there are some qualitative researchers who adopt these methods because they totally reject the positivism which has dominated research in the world for centuries (and still does), there are a great many who select methods appropriate for their research, sometimes quantitative, sometimes qualitative, and occasionally both. The subject matter often dictates the nature of the research. Investigating aspects of working memory, for example, would be terribly difficult if you chose a qualitative method, because people are generally not able to articulate memory processes very well. However, studying attitudes to spirituality within a personal context is unlikely to be achieved using an experimental method, or indeed any method which yields numbers.

One crucial aspect which may determine your choice of method is the 'richness' of the data. Generally, qualitative work produces 'richer' data than quantitative research. By 'richness', researchers usually mean that the data can provide deeper and often emotional insights into the processes and notions being researched. If you really want to get at the thoughts and feelings of your participants on a particular issue, you ought to be considering a qualitative method and analysis. Don't forget that qualitative analysis can stem from written texts, not just interviews. It is possible to take written answers to questions asked and subject them to a qualitative analysis. Most of the time, however, you are likely to conduct interviews to which you then apply a method such as discourse analysis or grounded theory.

Of course, qualitative methods come in many forms. Selecting one of these is sometimes a matter of the researcher's personal preferences, and in addition there are many debates between qualitative researchers as to which method is the best. Some researchers change methods depending upon the research, others stick to one only, and some try to blend methods in one piece of research. Most of the time, student projects involve just one well-established method.

This, as you are aware, is not a book on research methods, and so it is not appropriate here to give details of different qualitative approaches, but I have tried to make a few practical points about various qualitative trends in research.

- **Qualitative approaches are not just methods of analysis. They are entire philosophies about the way that research can and should be carried out.** Therefore, you should never try to 'tag on' a qualitative analysis to a quantitative project. Furthermore, never say something like 'the data were subjected to a grounded theory analysis'. The whole project needs to be based in grounded theory, not just the analysis.
- **Content Analysis:** to some academics, this is not really a qualitative method at all, but people sometimes talk about it as if it is, so be warned. It *can* be qualitative, but can also take you off into the realms of numbers as you begin to analyse patterns in data, and hunt for meaning in those patterns.
- **Protocol Analysis:** this is a type of qualitative approach leading from the method of introspection in cognitive psychology. It is a kind of bridge between qualitative and quantitative methods. It is only used where you want a different kind of perspective on the way that people go about things, such as solving problems. If you like cognitive psychology, but you like qualitative methods, this is a way of combining your interests.
- **Thematic Analysis:** this is a fairly basic approach which corresponds in some way to the first stages of the more complicated methods such as

grounded theory. It is not always a good way to achieve great marks because it can be a little simplistic at times.

- **Grounded Theory**: it is often difficult to conduct proper grounded theory in the context of a student project, especially where a proposal or literature review is required before commencing the research. One of the principles of grounded theory is that the ideas emerge from the data. You start as a naïve researcher, if possible. Therefore, it is generally recommended that you don't read all the literature before beginning. This can be tricky when you are being asked to do so. Be warned that a good grounded theory project can take a lot of time to do properly, especially because it normally involves going back and forth, generating ideas and following them up with more and more interviews until you feel that you haven't got anything left to say, and neither have your participants.

- **Ethnographic Methods**: these involve experiencing rather than observing. This can be difficult for a student to do. An ethnographic researcher discovers what it is to be a gambler by becoming one, or learns to understand the world of shoe retail by getting a job as a footwear salesperson. You would be advised to avoid the kind of ethnography which would involve you getting tied up with a world you might find it hard to escape from or which would affect you adversely. However, if you really wanted to try to tie in a new part-time job with your project in an interesting way, this *could* be possible. In addition, ethnography is about trying to interpret everyday life and the things we normally don't reflect on, not things which are out of the ordinary. Of course, different things make up ordinary, everyday life for different people.

- **Discourse Analysis**: this is not a single method, but many methods under one huge umbrella. Discourse analysis allows you to examine the nature of the way that discourses, or texts, are constructed by the language that we use to represent them. The language we use is not just seen as a tool to describe what is happening; it *is* what is happening. It has a strong political force behind it, in that we often are looking at the way we construct the world around us and the power relations that we develop to substantiate our involvement and our stake in various discourses. Discourse analysts don't usually try to suggest that the discourse is representing some deeper feelings or thoughts. The discourse is what everything is made of. You say something, which is a text. I think about what you mean, creating another text. This process is endless, but the texts are all that we have. It is hard work: be warned.

- Interpretative Phenomenological Analysis (IPA): an increasingly popular approach to qualitative psychology, especially within the study of health beliefs and cognitions. It deals with understanding the experience of a person, making the assumption that what they say reveals their deeper thoughts. In this sense it is quite different from discourse analysis (Smith, Jarman & Osborn, 1999). IPA is rapidly becoming the qualitative method of choice for health psychologists in particular, but can be used in any branch of research. It is possible to adapt the methods of the originators of the type of approach, as long as the main philosophical stance is preserved, which is that people's reported experiences and conversations can actually reveal their 'real' thoughts.
- Poststructuralist or Postmodern Methods: for most students, such methods are out of bounds because they are often very difficult to carry off properly. You need to be very *au fait* with what postmodernists think and feel, and because postmodernists reject being tied down to very much at all, you can easily get lost and feel like you are not actually doing research in the conventional sense. In fact, some supervisors might object to you carrying out some of the more esoteric postmodern methods, which could, in theory, include writing up your research in the form of a poem!
- Repertory Grid Technique: repertory grids are ways of exploring the way that people see their world, and themselves, and themselves in relation to their world. By identifying scenarios, and thoughts about scenarios, and by expressing ideas about other people, the participants (and the researchers) gain access to some of the ideas they possess about themselves. There can be some ethical issues surrounding the use of repertory grids because they can hold a metaphorical mirror up to people, revealing to them things which they did not realise they thought. Therefore, you should undertake this kind of work only in certain contexts and your proposal will be likely to be subject to careful, ethical scrutiny.

It is important to stress that you should not automatically seek to conduct a qualitative project because you dislike statistics or think that it will be easier than a quantitative one. It almost certainly won't be easier, I promise, and the amount of time you spend on a qualitative project is, if anything, likely to be more than that which you spend on a quantitative one. The difference in time could be used for brushing up your statistical knowledge! Of course, this is not meant to put you off conducting qualitative research, simply to warn you if you are thinking of doing it for the wrong reasons.

Differences or Relationships?

One of the important issues to think about is whether you intend looking at differences between groups or at relationships between variables that you have measured. As you should know, differences lead into analyses such as ANOVA, whereas relationships are analysed using correlation or regression. What you might not realise is that *sometimes* your study could turn out to involve either or both of these. As an example, consider a situation where you intend looking at problem-solving as a function of age and IQ. You have problem-solving scores from your participants, and you have their ages and IQ scores. Now, the most sensitive analysis would be to carry out a multiple regression predicting problem-solving scores from the other two variables. However, it is also possible to group ages and IQs. If you did this, perhaps into three groups of each (young, middle, older and low, middle, high), you could then fit this into an ANOVA. Statisticians would strongly recommend the regression analysis rather than the ANOVA, but if you were concerned about not having a good range of scores in your data for each variable then the ANOVA would be appropriate. I raise this because it makes the point that you should try to design certain studies so that you use continuous variables wherever possible. Aim for that, and if you get gaps in your data you can always switch analysis later. If you simply aim for categorical labelling of participants from the start you can't switch to the more sensitive regression analysis in the future.

One more issue you should remember is that of causality. Regression does not allow you to suggest that one thing actually causes another, because it is simply an extended form of correlation. ANOVA usually does, because it is an analysis that can be tied to the experimental method, where you have manipulated a set of independent variables to look for their effects on a dependent variable. However, the study described above is not truly experimental because the IQ and ages of the participants are not actually manipulated. Therefore, you should be thinking hard about the conclusions you want to make about your data and whether your method and your analysis will allow you to answer the questions you have.

Primary or Secondary Data?

Primary data are those that you have collected yourself, whereas secondary data originate elsewhere. Departments differ in their opinion of students using secondary data. However, generally, you will find that you are expected to collect primary data when using quantitative methods, but that secondary data are more acceptable when you are using a qualitative method. This is because there are certain common aspects of qualitative research which involve only secondary data, such as the study of TV or newspaper discourses. If you want to understand the nature of the representation of Romany people on TV, you wouldn't make your own TV programmes! You would use those which exist, and they would form your (secondary) data.

Observational Methods

Sometimes, the most appropriate method is an observational one. This is very often the case in any research into aspects of either social or developmental psychology. For example, you might want to research proxemics in a cross-cultural light. Proxemics is the study of personal distance, for example how close to each other people stand or sit. If you happen to have links with another culture, you could compare the average distance between British people in a queue with the queuing distance for Greek people, for instance. You would probably only consider doing this by employing an observational method.

Similarly, a developmental psychologist might be interested in some aspect of children's play behaviour. Again, you can't manipulate play directly, since you are likely to interfere with normal processes, and so you would best tackle this topic by observation.

Observational studies require considerable planning. The key issue is in making operational definitions of the behaviours concerned. You need to be very clear, before you commence the study, what you are actually observing and how you are coding and recording it. Observed behaviour can be very erratic at times, and you should have a coding scheme which covers almost all predictable eventualities. This is particularly important if you are observing things as they happen. Unless you are able to code everything that you see which is relevant, you will end up missing some important events. There is not the time to consult your supervisor when things start to happen that you haven't got any code for.

You should not underestimate the time that it will take to codify a small amount of videotape. Even five minutes of tape could take several hours to fully codify, depending on the complexity of your coding scheme.

You should set aside considerable time for piloting your observational research, and this should include a check on the reliability of your coding decisions. Just because you think that ten minutes into a videotape you spot an example of someone solving a problem by lateral thinking does not mean that someone else would agree. Therefore, when you have a pilot videotape to work from, code a part of it and then ask someone else to spend an hour or so going over the same portion of the tape. Then compare your results. If there is a high level of agreement you probably have a reasonable coding scheme and can continue to use it. If you don't agree, you will need to rethink the coding scheme since it is likely that it is subject to bias and not as objective as you would hope.

Similarly, if you are observing in the raw, without recording, ask someone to come along with you and make observations at the same time as you. Again, if you find that you are agreeing most of the time, then you can assume that you have a relatively objective method of measurement.

Protocol Analysis

Protocol analysis is a method of understanding cognitive processes which is generally subject to a qualitative analysis. In some ways it spans the chasm between quantitative and qualitative approaches. It has its roots in the method of introspection which was used in the early days of cognitive psychology. Essentially, participants articulate, out loud, their thought processes as they solve problems, and researchers analyse the resulting transcripts for evidence of particular problem-solving approaches, perhaps mapping these on to the theories derived from mainly experimental studies. Although protocol analysis is a relatively minor method, it can be a good one, and certainly ought to be considered if you want to investigate what people are thinking when they perform tasks.

Bear in mind that protocol analysis is hard work, and sometimes can be more difficult than either experimental or standard qualitative study. It cannot be used when cognitive processes are so quick that they are over in less than a few seconds, because the participants will have nothing to say. It is best used where the problems being solved take minutes or even hours. There is also the problem of the 'language epiphenomenon' to consider. Just because someone says they are thinking something does not mean that this is actually going on. They might be telling the truth as far as they are concerned, but the thought processes are often generally going on at a level below consciousness, with the protocols being only a representation of that which is fed into consciousness. This problem is probably the main reason why protocol analysis is not the most popular method of understanding cognitive processes.

Multiple Methods

In some research, using more than one method might be a good approach. Addressing a problem in more than one way can be very revealing. We often call this triangulation. If more than one method achieves the same results, we can say that we have triangulated our findings. In the past, I have seen some very good projects where the student has conducted a questionnaire survey (with a quantitative analysis) and then followed this up with some interviews involving qualitative analysis. Often, the same thing comes out of both approaches. You feel more confident in your results if you can show that they are present no matter how you look at the subject. However, some qualitative methods are derived from a tradition which is absolutely opposed to the concept of triangulation, so you need to take this into account so that you don't try fitting a square peg into a round hole.

⌗ CONTROL GROUPS

Throughout your studies, you will generally have been taught that it is wise to include a control group in most research designs. Theoretically, it is true that control groups are useful and represent an ideal which you should always consider. However, it is not always practical to include a control group, and sometimes it does not even make sense to pursue such a course of action.

In studies where you are interested in a particular group of people, you can often discount including any kind of control group. This can happen when you are conducting interview research into the thoughts and feelings of a certain subset of the population. If you want to know what Pakistani people feel about unemployment, then ask them. You would only ask other people if you specifically wanted to compare Pakistani people with another group. Another example could be where you are interested in how doctors come to diagnostic conclusions. In such a case, it is only doctors who formally make such decisions, and so understanding how people who are not doctors diagnose illness is absurd.

More controversially, there are other kinds of studies where you do not necessarily require a control group. Although academics would debate this, occasionally you can also skip a control group in more experimental studies. If you want to look at the effects of caffeine on motor performance, it can be argued that you don't need a non-caffeine group, as long as you have more than one dosage of caffeine being given to participants. If you expect caffeine to speed up performance, you might have three caffeine groups: mild, moderate, and strong dose. If you find an increase in participants' speed across the three groups, then it is difficult to argue that it is not due to caffeine, and so the control group is, one could suggest, unnecessary. The control group is probably no more necessary than some additional caffeine groups. Some researchers would counter-argue, and rightly so, that you can't be sure of the point at which caffeine starts to have an effect unless you have a control no-caffeine group. By looking at the comparison between the control and the treatment groups you can get a sense of how much caffeine you actually need before you notice a difference beyond that observed when caffeine is not involved. Bear in mind, therefore, that excluding a control group is essentially a cost-cutting exercise, and you should not do it unless you have to.

♯ MATCHING METHODS TO ANALYSIS

You should never carry out research until you are utterly sure of what analysis you can conduct when the data are collected. It is very easy to plan some research which is actually impossible to analyse, or only possible to analyse if you have carefully stratified your samples and have thousands of participants! When you are excited about some research, you have a tendency to think deeply about it and come up with dozens of variables which you feel you really must measure if you are to find out what you want. The more you read about a subject, the more you think of things which are important to study. However, every time you add a variable or measure to a study you complicate the analysis and increase the number of participants you need to recruit. Therefore, you might find that you take a rather large and straggly idea to your supervisor, who then takes a pair of clippers and snips away until you are left with something much neater and more manageable. In fact, going to see your supervisor is often like a visit to the hairdresser. Their job is to trim and shape what you have, to advise you against doing something you might regret, and you tend to feel better when you leave.

Always keep in mind, when you are planning research, what your data will look like, and exactly what kind of analysis (statistical or otherwise) you are going to feed the data into. This is mainly an issue for quantitative projects, but can affect any research.

If you plan research carefully, there is no reason why you cannot find a suitable analysis or set of analyses to perform, and your supervisor is there to make sure that you don't collect data that you can't do anything with. Always remember, however, that when it comes to quantitative work, particularly experiments, you should really only conduct statistical analysis which is directly aimed at answering the questions raised by your hypotheses. If you later go fishing around in your data you could end up finding things which aren't really there. Statistical tests are designed to help you to answer specific questions, not to enable you to trawl around sets of numbers until you find something.

♯ POWER ANALYSIS

Although this is not a book on statistics, it is relevant to mention power analysis here, since it should help to inform your research plans. In my own experience, it is very common for students to talk through a piece of research and then ask a very particular question at the end: 'So how many participants should I get?'

Power analysis can be used to answer this very question. Almost all statistics book give details of this kind of predictive analysis, and it can be used to give you an idea of the sample size you might need. You can even find shareware programs on the internet which will calculate sample size required if you can set a desired level of power and estimate of effect size.

If you are conducting research which involves co-operation with a hospital, or general practitioner, for which you need to submit your research to an external ethics committee, you will almost certainly have to conduct a power analysis to determine your sample size. This is for a good reason. Ethics committees like to be sure that you only deal with the minimum number of people for the study to be effective. Otherwise you are pestering people for nothing. Therefore, a power analysis helps to show just how many people you need to have involved in your study, and it stops you collecting data that are superfluous.

♯ DEVELOPING MATERIALS

It is not possible to give specific tips as to how to set up every type of material that you might conceivably use. The potential for developing materials is infinite. However, there are some general rules that you should follow when creating interview schedules, constructing questionnaires, making up stimuli and so on.

Experimental Stimuli

Stimuli for experimental studies can be extremely difficult to create. Mostly, such stimuli are created for specific kinds of experiment, those conducted by cognitive psychologists interested in the nature of the mental lexicon or in how we perceive objects. Stimuli come in a number of modalities. They can be auditory, visual, or even olfactory or gustatory. Frequently, they take the form of lists of words and non-words. You are often interested in people's reaction times when responding to these stimuli.

Let us take, as an example, a lexical decision task. Here the participants must decide whether the text presented on a screen is either a word or a non-word. In constructing the stimuli, you must consider a number of things.

- The words you choose will probably have to have certain characteristics. You might only want nouns, or only verbs, for example. You should also consider their frequency in the English language. In a lexical decision task, you would normally want fairly common words because if you use rare words there is a chance that your participants simply won't have heard of them. You can't decide if something is a word if you have never heard of it. You can consult special books of word frequencies from which you can extract stimuli. Your library may have one of these, or some can be found on the internet. They are usually called something like a 'word-frequency corpus'. Consider also using the stimuli that someone else has already constructed. You will commonly find lists of these in the appendices of relevant articles.
- You will need as many non-words as words. Not only this, but they should be matched with the words you are using for length, and possibly other characteristics such as initial letter. Usually they will have to be what are called pseudo-words. These look like words but aren't, for example 'spung'. This is because a random string of letters (such as 'drpuig') is immediately recognisable as a non-word, but a pseudo-word isn't. You don't want the task to be too easy for the participants.
- You need to consider how many stimuli you will need. If you have too many, participants will lose concentration. If you have too few, then you will be left with even fewer responses on which to base your analysis, especially after trimming the data to remove any outliers. Furthermore, as you will realise, the more stimuli you have the greater chance that you will be genuinely tapping the ability of the participant

and the more confident you can be in the results of your study. There is no magic formula for deciding how many stimuli to have, which is one reason why you should conduct a pilot study. However, you should aim for a task which does not take more than about five minutes for your participant to complete.

- You should think about whether you want all stimuli presented in a long block, or whether you can give your participant a number of smaller blocks.
- You should avoid patterns in the presentation of stimuli which could lead participants astray in responding. This is especially a problem when using smaller numbers of stimuli and relying on a computer to present them. If you have words and non-words, and you allow the computer to randomly present stimuli plucked from each set, you could find that a sequence of presentations all come from one category, such as words. So your participants are faced with seven real words one after the other. When this kind of thing happens, your participants sometimes get distracted, and wonder if something has gone wrong. Or, you might get a sequence where words alternate with non-words. Such sequences are rare, but can happen in randomly generated lists. To avoid this, researchers often rely on what is called a pseudorandom sequence. Some computer programmes will allow you to do this. Instead of a genuine random presentation where anything could happen, you make sure that these patterns of stimuli do not occur. So, you might choose to allow no more than three stimuli from a particular category to be presented, for example. The participants do not know this, and feel like the stimuli are being randomly presented, but the order of presentation is not truly random because you have tinkered with it a little.
- Don't forget to have some stimuli left over when you have constructed your lists in order that you can set up a practice trial. You should never use your real stimuli in the practice trial, because priming effects can occur.

Check with your departmental technicians, because they might surprise you and have a store of useful stimuli to hand, either from previous research projects, or even commercially obtained ones.

Questionnaires

Often it will be entirely appropriate for you to take tests straight 'off the shelf' and use them. However, sometimes you will be creating your own questionnaire. The first thing to note is that you cannot, realistically, develop a questionnaire which will have the same high degree of validity and reliability as published ones. Published tests and questionnaires have been through many versions in their development, and have usually been tried out on hundreds and often thousands of respondents. However, you should still aim to follow the normal procedures for constructing questionnaires, even if you do everything on a much smaller scale.

If you do need to create a new questionnaire, begin by simply thinking of questions off the top of your head. Write down as many as you can. Furthermore, you might like to ask some friends for their ideas as well. Occasionally other people can have surprising insights into the kind of thing you are researching, even when they are not psychologists.

Imagine that you want to create a questionnaire to measure emotionality. By this, we might mean the tendency for some people to feel things very strongly and for others to feel them less so. We all know people who are 'touchy' or 'soft' and who might cry at the drop of a hat. Then there are those people who are 'as tough as old boots' or 'hard'. They never seem to cry or be affected by sob stories. There is no reason why you could not ask non-psychologists to think of examples of what being emotional means. Most people have an opinion on it, and could think of examples of it. You could also ask a few people you know who you would describe as emotional types. What makes them feel upset or happy might prove useful information to you. In the end, you should be able to construct a large number of potential questions. They might involve various scenarios such as being affected by sad stories on the news, being easily hurt by offhand remarks, being emotionally affected by films or poetry, and so on.

Try to create questions which ask just one thing each. That is, avoid double-barrelled questions where a person is not sure what they are agreeing to. If you ask someone if they think that alcohol is bad for the mind and the body, do you want to know if it is bad for the mind, the body or both? Surely it is better to ask both things separately?

Use simple language when writing questions. Try to imagine the least educated person you would be asking to participate, and make the questions clear to them. If you can do this, all participants will be able to answer your questions properly.

Think carefully about the nature of the measurement scales that you are using. Some questionnaires simply present statements which require a YES or NO answer. The number of answers is then totted up for each to give a total score. Others require responses on a Likert-type scale. Some contain a visual analogue scale where respondents must place a mark on a straight line to indicate the strength of their opinion. Try to stick to one type of scale, because it makes life easier for the respondent. Make sure that your respondents don't have to keep turning back to the front page in order to check the details of the response scale. Print the scale on each page, or, if relevant, beneath each individual item.

When you have questions about the importance of various things, think about asking your participants to rank those things in order. So, if you want to know what people think is the most important health behaviour from a list such as not smoking, eating fruit and vegetables, taking exercise, and so on, consider listing these and asking participants to respond by giving a number of importance to each one. This can be a neat technique for forcing people to compare various things, but be aware that it can also be a little artificial and should only be used when you know exactly what you want people to think about. You are suggesting all of the behaviours or attitudes to be ranked, and so you miss out on other things which you, perhaps, haven't thought of, but which are important to your respondents.

Always have more questions than you need. Some will have to be cut out in the later stages of constructing the questionnaire. If you intend having a questionnaire with 20 items in it, start the process with around 30–40 items. Pilot the questionnaire, and then check the internal reliability of each scale or sub-scale you have created by running a test such as Cronbach's alpha. Remove any questions which do not cohere with the rest, and aim for a high reliability coefficient (generally 0.8 or more). Remember that you only run Cronbach's alpha on questions which you believe are all asking the same type of thing. Don't just put every single question into the analysis. Additionally, ask your pilot participants to comment on the questions. You might find that what makes sense to you does not make sense to them.

Avoid 'acquiescence response bias' where possible. If you have a set of questions which are all worded in a particular way, people stop thinking about the questions and simply assume that because they have answered YES to all 17 so far they will be answering YES to the rest of them. This is a very dangerous situation because it compromises your entire research. It also bores the pants off your participants if they never have to think and reflect on your questions. You can try to avoid this by rephrasing some of your questions so that they require a reversal of the scale. In the case of YES/NO responses, imagine the following:

- I like the human race. YES/NO.
- I enjoy a night out with friends. YES/NO.
- There's nothing better than a lively party. YES/NO.

Imagine you were presented with 20 such statements. If you generally are a sociable and philanthropic person, you will probably answer YES to all of them. However, you should try to aim for at least one-third of your questions pointing to a NO response. So, we can rephrase all of these questions and effectively turn them around, thus:

- I dislike the human race. YES/NO.
- I do not enjoy a night out with friends. YES/NO.
- There's nothing worse than a lively party. YES/NO.

Now the sociable person is required to answer NO. By mixing questions of this nature, you make sure that your respondents have to think about each question.

Eventually you ought then to have a questionnaire which is almost usable. Of course, at this point you can't guarantee that you have high validity, unless you have tested your questionnaire against existing ones which aim to assess the same thing. It should be said, however, that if a questionnaire already exists you would have probably used that one instead of going to the trouble of creating your own.

Make sure you include some demographic questions at the head of your questionnaire, unless you really don't need them. However, if you don't ask these questions you lose the chance of looking for age or sex effects later, for example, should you wish to explore this in your data. There are two things to keep your eye on with respect to asking your respondents' ages. First, if you insist on asking people to choose an age category, make sure they don't overlap! I have frequently seen first drafts of questionnaires where the age categories are 20–30, 30–40, 40–50, and so on. Of course, if you happen to be exactly 30, or exactly 40, you have a choice of two categories! This error ought not to occur, however. The reason is because you ought not to be asking for age in categories. Why not simply ask people to give their exact age in years? That way you have a much more sensitive measure of age, which you might want to use in regression analyses, for example. If you really want to categorise age you can do it later.

A good questionnaire contains the minimum number of items to find out what you are interested in. People groan when you hand them a weighty questionnaire to fill in, and so you should try to make your respondents' lives as easy as possible. Of course, too few items could mean that you aren't really digging out the information that you need, or rather you aren't adequately sampling the attitudes that you want to learn more about. It's not possible to give a formula for the optimum length of questionnaires, but you should always time your participants in your pilot study to get a sense of how long it is taking them to fill in your paperwork. Generally, any more than 30 minutes and you are probably going to annoy your respondents.

Looking Professional

The way that your questionnaire or instructions are presented can be very important in conveying a sense of professionalism. Well-presented materials, especially clear questionnaires which are pleasing to the eye, can add to the quality of the data you collect. When people see that you are serious and intelligent, they take you seriously and show you their intelligence too. Shoddily presented questionnaires full of mistakes of spelling and grammar do not inspire confidence.

Although you are not a designer, you should always take a moment to look at the design of your questionnaire. Does it look 'posh' and 'fancy', or something that a beginner has thrown together in a matter of minutes? Now, posh and fancy does not mean using bizarre typefaces which are difficult to read, or including unnecessary pictures, but it does mean having clear text, having just the right amount of text on each page, and tidying up the text so that it looks as much like something you would find in a book as possible.

- Justify the text on both sides of the page.
- Make sure that headings are emboldened so that they are clear.
- Put spaces between questions, and make sure that there is the same amount of space between each item.
- Give respondents enough room to give their response, whether it be a tick box or a blank space for writing comments.
- Number the pages so that people realise if there is a page missing.
- Show everything to your supervisor before you distribute it, so they can help to spot errors and omissions.
- Check what you print off before you photocopy it for distribution. Just because something looks good on screen does not mean that it will print properly.
- When you want to equally space items across the page, don't use the space bar to move things along. The space is a character just like a letter. Your word-processing package is likely to adjust the size of spaces depending upon the rest of the text on the line, thus messing up your spacing. Use proper tabulation which you can set, or put the

items into columns in a table. You can hide tables by removing the lines around them, so that when they are printed you can't see them. The text in them stays in place, however.

Interviews

Many of the issues surrounding constructing good items in a questionnaire survey also apply to the questions you would generate for use in an interview. However, interviews also have their own issues to be borne in mind.

In the case of interviews, the material takes the form of the interview schedule. Some methods of qualitative work do not involve the use of a schedule, since the aim is to simply allow the interviewee to talk freely without prompts. However, the majority of methods do involve a schedule, or some indication of the likely questions, loose as that may be.

It is often not easy to generate questions which will actually serve the intended purpose. You must aim to encourage your interviewee, whilst not leading them to give you the answers that you want. Leading questions are not acceptable. You must be clear. Equally, you must not give too much away. The worst problem that you can face is when you have an interviewee who is simply not forthcoming. There is a temptation when this happens to blame them, ascribing the problem to their shyness or awkwardness. However, you must not do this. If someone is not saying much, it's because you are not doing your job properly. If you have taken the trouble to prepare properly this should happen very rarely. Your questions should not be of the type where it is possible for people to simply utter 'yeah', 'suppose so', or 'no'. This very problem is why you should practise your interview technique. Basically, you need to conduct a pilot study, primarily to ensure that you have the necessary skills to actually conduct a good interview. You must make the interviewees comfortable, willing to talk, and happy to be honest. Different kinds of people require different interview techniques to get the best out of them, and you must be adaptable whilst working within the constraints of your research and sticking to the subject at hand.

A good way to see if you have prepared an effective interview schedule is to try it out on your least talkative friend. Don't pick the gabby one who will talk about the inside of a ping-pong ball for an hour. Choose the quiet one.

One increasingly common type of questioning is sometimes known as the *narrative approach*. Rather than ask people direct questions, you ask them to tell you about something that has happened to them. They end up telling you a short story selected from their experiences, and they simply can't answer abruptly and briefly because of the nature of the question asked. Narrative questions are quite easy to construct, and are often like these:

- Tell me about a time when you treated yourself to something nice.
- Could you tell me about an occasion when you felt cheated by someone?
- Can you describe a situation you found yourself in that you learned something from?

Be prepared to follow up these questions, however, if your interviewee is confused by your question. I can remember the very first time that I was interviewed using this approach. The researcher started the tape recorder and then said something like "tell me about relationships". I didn't know what to say. I didn't know where to begin, or whether I would start talking only for her to stop me and say that I was not talking about the 'right' things. My question to her was "What about them? Could you ask me something a little more specific so I know what you are interested in finding out?" So, bear this in mind. Anyone who knows me will tell you that I can normally talk the hind legs off a donkey, but I was rendered speechless to begin with.

Cross-cultural Studies and Translation of Materials

Generally, you are unlikely to be interested in conducting cross-cultural studies unless you have some personal involvement in more than one culture or ethnicity, mainly because you need to have intimate knowledge of some cultures in order to even think about studying them. Quite a few students do have this joint background, however, and in my experience such students often conduct some interesting and valuable research. In Britain, there are particularly strong communities from the Indian subcontinent, from China and Hong Kong, and from African countries and the Caribbean. Furthermore, substantial numbers of students from Europe also choose to study in Britain. Often, students with relevant family histories choose to investigate various aspects of their family cultures. One key issue for all cross-cultural studies is that of translation of materials. If you are using questionnaires or other test materials you will often need to translate them into another language. Without boring you with all of the theory of interpretation and translation, which is a whole area of study in itself, there are a few things you need to remember.

Don't translate things word-for-word. Translation is all about conveying meaning. Therefore, you need to consider what your materials in English actually are aiming to achieve, and attempt to create translated materials which have the same objectives. Most of the time you can translate things quite easily, but now and then you will, perhaps, have to drop certain items because they do not travel well from one language to another. Equally, what might be a perfectly good question to ask the average British person might be utterly rude to ask a person from Pakistan. Be very careful that you consider all of this.

When you have translated your materials into another language, find someone else who is fluent in both relevant languages, and get them to 'back-translate'. So, you will end up with a second version in the original language. Then compare yours with theirs. They should be similar, and if they are not, you need to consider what you are going to do about it. Discuss this with the other person, and see if there is any agreement you can come to. If you really can't agree on a translation, then there is a possibility that you need to reconsider your research.

⊞ 'BORROWING' MATERIALS

Whether it be questionnaires or lists of stimuli or photographs, you might be able to use the materials previously developed by other researchers. When you read a research article, there will sometimes be an appendix containing the materials. This usually means that you are able to use them yourself without any special permission, but always check with your supervisor.

If this is not the case, you could try getting in touch with the authors of the article, politely asking them about the availability of their materials. Look at the list of authors at the head of the piece. Normally, the first author is the one you should try to contact, and it will usually be indicated if not. If an email address is not given, you can probably track the authors down via the internet, because you will certainly know where they are based (unless they have moved on since the article was published). If you write to them, do so with respect and politeness, and mention that you are a student. Ask them if their materials are 'in the public domain' and, if so, whether they will allow you to use them. If you are lucky, they'll send you what you need. You might even find that they are interested in your results. Make sure that you thank them in your Acknowledgements section. Finally, show your supervisor the email you intend sending just in case there is any problem. (Now and then, supervisors prefer to make contact with the authors on your behalf. Don't be offended if this is the case. They might know the people concerned, and might want to phrase a letter to them in a particular way. After all, you probably wouldn't write a letter to your grandparents in the same style as one to an old friend.)

⌗ THE INTERNET AS A RESEARCH TOOL

It is becoming increasingly popular for people to use the internet as a place for hosting surveys, in order to maximise response rates and generate a wider and more representative sample. Psychologists are in debate over the validity of using the internet for research. My own advice is that generally you should not use it, because I believe that the problems outweigh the benefits. There are a few issues you must consider before uploading your survey questionnaires:

- Don't put anything out there which requires a timed response. Too much relies on the timing of internet connections rather than the actual response times of the participants.
- Be aware that internet users are a restricted sample of the general public, despite the fact that the internet is becoming increasingly commonplace. The oldest and poorest people in society are the least likely to have internet access. Furthermore, internet users who have managed to stumble on to your survey and then agree to fill it in are an even more specific subset of the population.
- Be prepared to accept that some people are just awkward and like to ruin research for the sake of it. Hackers may take pleasure from breaking into your html code and spoiling things, some people will complete your survey a number of times under different names, and some people will give ridiculous answers because it amuses them. People can just as easily 'spoil' a pen-and-paper version, although the anonymity of the internet is more likely to encourage this. People tend to take you more seriously if you have handed them a questionnaire personally.
- One of the biggest problems with web-based instruments is that they need to be somewhere on the internet where people will actually encounter them. Even then there is no guarantee that they will take part. Unless you have access to some popular internet site (perhaps your friend runs a site which clocks up thousands of hits per day and on which they are happy to host your questionnaire), you should think

about the amount of work you would have to put in to create an online questionnaire which no-one might ever find!

My best suggestion to get around most of these problems is this. You should not rely solely on the internet, but conduct a pen-and-paper survey as well. Then, when the data are in, compare the two forms, checking your survey item by item, running statistical tests to see if the internet version is significantly different from the pen-and-paper one. If the responses match up, then you can consider adding the lot together and working on it as if everything had been from a single source. If you find that the answers are often quite different, you must consider trusting the pen-and-paper one more.

⌗ MANAGING TIME: KEEPING ON TRACK

One of the biggest problems students face when engaging with research is managing their time so that deadlines are met and the research does not spill over into other things. Even when your department is happy to provide you with an extension for your project, you might find that this means that there is less time for you to get ready for your final examinations. Therefore, it is important that you avoid, wherever possible, having to ask for extensions to deadlines. Plan your time carefully, and the time will serve you well.

Start Early

The most important advice you can be given is to start early. Usually, you have a whole summer before you must get started on your project. If you can make good use of that time, you will have a head start on other students in your year, most of whom don't really get going until the early months of the academic year. Even when your lecturers try to get you thinking about your project early (such as at the end of your penultimate year), many students still hold back and leave things until the final year begins.

Match the Project to the Time Available

Most students have around six months to complete a project. Obviously, this is the figure you need to start with. Therefore, many longitudinal projects are ruled out because of this. If you trim the six months to include time for planning, piloting, analysis and writing up, you can be left with as little as three months to actually conduct the research. This means that there is a severe limitation on any longitudinal work you intend to do. If you are following up participants every week for three months, you end up with 12 points of data collection, which is probably fine. However, if you intend collecting data on something which might change very slowly over time, you could find that nothing is likely to happen even in three whole months. If that's a likely outcome, then the research simply can't be done in the timescale you have available and you need to rethink. For the vast majority of student projects, however, including those with a longitudinal focus, three months is probably long enough to get a decent piece of research work done. One thing is certain, though; if you drag your heels it won't be.

Over-planning

Research almost always takes longer than you think. It is best, therefore, to overplan your time. By this, I mean that you should build some slack into your schedule. Expect things to go wrong, or data collection to hit an obstacle and slow down, and make allowance for this to happen. So, you will need to build in around ten to twenty per cent of additional time. You might not need it, but the worst that can happen if you don't is that you will finish early. If you don't expect things to go wrong, you'll be scrambling around towards the deadline.

In practice, this additional time must be shaved off the six months or so that you have. Six months is 24 weeks. A tenth of six months is nearly two-and-a-half weeks. As a minimum, in this case, you need to plan as if you had 21.5 weeks. If you are in any doubt yourself about access to participants, or if you know that you struggle with statistics, or if you are quite slow when it comes to writing up, I recommend that you build in the full 20 per cent of emergency time. That works out at almost five weeks. Therefore, plan for a project that you can conduct and complete within 19 weeks. This sounds dramatic, and depressing, but you can't always predict what might go wrong. It is better to be ready for an emergency than to risk making a mess of something really important to you.

Plan B

If you have any worries about how the project might pan out, then you should consider having a Plan B. Sometimes you are relying on someone else or another organisation to help you to have access to participants. Therefore, some of the things that could go wrong could be out of your hands. If your access to participants falls through, or if you don't find enough people to take part because of the nature of the study, you might need to cut your losses and switch plans. Plan B should not be a completely different project, but a new version of the original which might not be as interesting to you but is more likely to succeed in a short time. You should try to construct a Plan B which will mean that your literature searching is not wasted because you can use all of the same articles in your introduction. The theory should not dramatically change, just the nature of the data-collection process. A standard way to create a Plan B is to alter your study into a study of attitudes. Imagine that you wanted to look at coping strategies in people with cystic fibrosis (CF). Then you find that you won't be able to find enough people with CF to take part because of some practical obstacle. Instead, you could ask people who don't have the illness about how they would cope if it affected them. You give them information about the condition, and then they are asked about how they imagine they would deal with it themselves. There are all sorts of possibilities as to how you could then set about looking at this data. It's not ideal, but it's something you can get a project out of. Yes, it's true that there is a big difference between facing CF in your life and trying to imagine what you might feel like. In fact, these two things are worlds apart, but better that than you waste a lot of time and effort and be left with absolutely nothing at the end of it all.

If you have *some* people with CF involved in your study, but don't feel that you have enough, you can always shift the focus slightly into comparing two conditions. What you might do is find some other medical condition or illness which shares some characteristics with CF but is different in some key aspect, and then make your study one of comparison of coping in two different conditions. For example, CF is primarily something which affects the lungs, and so you might find another lung disease, such as emphysema, and then identify some relevant participants that way. As long as you have been prepared for this possibility all along you should find this a feasible way to proceed. Do note, however, that you will probably need ethical approval all over again should you switch to a Plan B.

Although it is not ideal, you can often consider adding a qualitative element to a quantitative project, or vice versa. Occasionally, it can be quite enlightening if you see if your results seem to hold true even when you change the method. If you have conducted a questionnaire survey, you can consider adding an interview or two which explores the same issues but in more depth. It would be highly unusual to add a quantitative element to a qualitative project, and many psychologists would strongly object to this, so if you consider this you must do so very carefully and only in consultation with your supervisor. In the case of qualitative projects, a better Plan B might be to revisit the people that you have interviewed and follow up specific points in an additional interview. You are much more likely to be able to follow up your participants than you are to find new ones.

Note that these are plans which should only be put into place if you are desperate because things have gone wrong. You should not resort to these unless you really need to.

Response Rates

If you are using questionnaires, you will need to plan your time and resources around likely response rates, especially if you are expecting replies by post. For example, you might be sending out a questionnaire with the newsletter of an organisation from whom you have permission. You hope that the members will fill them in and send them back to you. First, you must give people a long time to do this. Even though people may have the best of intentions, they can often forget about something for months on end. Secondly, you should be ready to spend/waste a lot of money on photocopying of questionnaires which will never be returned to you. A truly excellent response rate for questionnaires by post is around fifty per cent. Some studies actually end up with a return of less than one-tenth. So, realistically, you ought to expect around a third to come back to you, depending upon the nature of the questionnaire and the nature of the people to whom you are sending them. If you are targeting members of an automobile club with a questionnaire about driving behaviour you can expect a much higher rate than if you are asking members of a chess club to fill in questionnaires about their eating habits or their attitudes towards building development on 'brownfield' sites. Therefore, generally, print and send out 300 questionnaires for every 100 you want back. If you are sending out questionnaires cold, i.e. to people who have not shown any interest in your study in any way, then you will be lucky if you get five back out of every hundred, which means that this is not a practicable method at all.

Now, here's something for you to ponder. According to Sommer & Sommer (2002, p.151) 'Some market researchers believe that a stamp placed at a slight angle on the envelope increases the return rate.'

Your Supervisor's Time

Many students have a tendency to forget, sometimes, that their supervisor has demands on his or her time as well. In an average university, a project supervisor is usually working with a number of students on their projects. In addition, your supervisor is likely to be involved in teaching, preparing materials for various courses or modules, writing, and research; may have doctoral students to supervise; meetings to attend; marking to do; new courses to develop; involvement with their professional body; and external examining commitments to fulfil at other universities. They also have to sleep and find time to take their holidays. As a result, you need to plan your use of their time as much as your own. Make appointments with your supervisor well in advance. Don't forget to attend them, and if you need to cancel, again do so in plenty of time, as a matter of courtesy. Your demands on your supervisor's time tend to be quite predictable; generally you will need quite a bit of their time when you are planning the research, much less once you are collecting data, and then a sizeable chunk of your time allowance will be used up when you are understanding your data and analysis and writing up. Therefore, plan accordingly. Remember, too, that when you most need your supervisor, that is, in the last few weeks before handing in your completed project, they will be trying to fit all of their other equally frantic students in as well. If you leave things to the last minute, you may well find that your supervisor cannot find the time to see you because other people have used up their time. To avoid this, you need a very good idea of when you will be needing your supervisor and you should try to make appointments which match your predictions.

Project Milestones

You might not be familiar with something called a Gantt chart. Essentially, it is a map of time. Table 1 is an example of a small one. It should be obvious at a glance what it tells you. When you start your research, create one, and show it to your supervisor, who can then (a) check that you do have a realistic time plan and (b) be impressed because you are organised!

Different types of project will usually require completely different Gantt charts, because some research is 'data collection heavy', whilst being 'analysis light'. Other types of research are just the opposite. Usually, this is the big difference between quantitative and qualitative

Table 1   A Fictitious Research Project Gantt Chart

	October	November	December	January	March	April
Planning	▓	▓				
Piloting		▓				
Writing Introduction		▓				
Writing Method			▓			
Writing Discussion					▓	▓
Data collection			▓	▓		
Analysis				▓	▓	

work. Interviewing a handful of people can be very quick and easy if you are good at it, but transcribing and coding the interviews is long-winded and time-consuming. However, collecting data from hundreds of participants in a quantitative study can take hundreds of hours, but the analysis can take seconds using a computer program.

Tips on Managing Time

There are entire books and management courses devoted to managing time. It never fails to amuse me that the biggest problem in managing my own time always seems to be that I never have the time to sit down and methodically manage my time. However, your project is very important to you, and so you should consider sparing an hour or so to put your working life in order and make sure that your academic year does not speed past you, leaving you wondering where it all went.

- Break the writing-up into small chunks and deal with each separately. This is easy to do because research is reported in sections anyway.
- Make a list of things to do. Some people do this daily, but weekly will usually suffice. Cross things off as you do them and notice how much better you feel as the list for the week starts to shrink.
- Don't stare at a pile of work or list of chores and depress yourself at how big it is. Mountain climbers work in stages. A walk around the earth begins with the first step. If you feel overwhelmed by things to do, do some of them and you will have made a start. You will feel better. Just

don't see your list of tasks as a great monster staring at you; it's really just a crowd of tiny monsters!

• Start tackling a list of chores by choosing the most pleasurable or easiest of them and getting that out of the way. Then deal with the worst one after you have warmed up, leaving some more of the easier tasks to deal with at the end when you are more tired.

• Plan breaks in your work time. Not only should you aim to have a day off every now and then, you should also plan to have smaller breaks regularly throughout the working day. If you are stumped by a problem, or if you have writer's block, a small break will often help and the problem sometimes goes away just because you have taken a rest.

• Try to estimate how long everything you have to do will take you, and then keep your eye on the clock. You will often be surprised at how wrong you are about how long things take. Many things look as if they might take hours and are done in minutes, but the converse also applies.

• Although not everyone is the same, most people have a couple of peak periods for work each day, and a couple of lulls when they are at their worst. Usually, the lulls come after lunch (for biological reasons) and early in the morning (when the body and mind are still waking up). The peaks tend to be in the late morning and the late afternoon/early evening. Find out when your peaks and troughs are. Then make sure that you tackle difficult tasks in your peaks, and save the mundane mindless tasks for your troughs.

• Clear your desk regularly. Scraps of paper not only get in the way of the things you actually need, they also make you feel as if things are in a mess.

• Don't throw anything away until your project is completely finished and you are certain that you won't need it again. File everything away for the time being.

• Don't stress yourself over the fact that time is ticking away. Everyone conducting a research project in your year is working to the same schedule, and time is very fair; a minute is the same length for everyone.

• Give yourself a treat at the end of a long working day. Whether you have a chocolate bar in the cupboard, or a film to watch, you will have something to look forward to.

⌗ WRITING A PROPOSAL

It is common for students to be asked to write a proposal for their research, which may or may not contribute to the marks awarded to the project, or the proposal may be marked in its own right as a piece of work. Normally, a research proposal is nothing to be afraid of. If you can imagine writing a research report without the results and discussion section, then you have a mental picture of what a proposal looks like. The only other real difference is that you will be writing about research to be conducted (future tense) rather than that which is now completed.

"MY INTERNET SEARCH
SAID THIS WAS A BOOK
ABOUT GROUNDED THEORY..."

A proposal is not a waste of time. It can help you to focus your ideas, but primarily can be the basis of your Introduction or Literature Review in your project proper. After all, if you have read dozens of articles to produce a rationale in your proposal, you can make use of that and tweak it to produce a real introduction to the research in your written-up project.

Commonly, proposals contain sections which might be labelled thus: literature review, Method, Proposed Analysis, Practical and Theoretical Applications, References. In the section that I have suggested could be called 'Practical Applications', you ought to explicitly state what the point of your study will be, i.e. what theories you will be adding to or rejecting and who is likely to benefit from your addition to knowledge. Remember to write the Methods of the proposal in the future tense, since you haven't started doing anything at this stage. This contrasts with using the past tense for a report write-up when the research is over.

⌗ RESEARCH ETHICS

Being a good psychology researcher means that you must have a sensitivity to the rights and wrongs of conducting research with human participants. In some senses, ethics are the first hurdle of carrying out worthwhile research. Most people *think* that they have a good sense of ethics, but it isn't that simple. Just because something seems OK to you does not mean that it is. This is the reason why most research has to be considered for approval by an ethics committee of some sort who make a joint decision. By debate, different opinions on what is right and what is wrong are likely to be aired. Top ethics committees are usually made up of a selection of academics, religious leaders (priests, mullahs, rabbis, and so on), heads of consumer organisations or pressure groups, and members of the public. However, the majority of research that students are doing can be overseen by a much less formal committee, often made up of members of psychology staff.

There are many codes of conduct which set out guidelines for conducting research. In Britain, the most commonly followed by psychologists are those created by the British Psychological Society (BPS). If your research does not fit within the BPS's *Code of Conduct, Ethical Principles & Guidelines* then you really will not be able to go ahead. Many of your lecturers will be members of the BPS, and so are expected to work within these guidelines as a matter of professional honour. You can get a copy of these from the BPS directly, including online from *www.bps.org.uk*. They are loosely summarised here for your convenience. You should be aware of these right from the start of your project because they should guide your choice of topic and how you will go about conducting your research. *Note that this summary of some of the main points of the Code of Conduct does not constitute a replacement or equivalent to the original document, and you are strongly advised to read the source document before beginning an investigation. The points listed below are simply my explanation of the issues you must consider and, as such, the wording is not officially endorsed by the BPS. Furthermore, the guidelines on work with animals are not included here, since the vast majority of student projects do not involve animal work; indeed, such work is often not allowed in psychology departments today. If you are permitted to pursue a project involving non-human participants, make sure that you are following the BPS Code of Conduct in this respect, and that you have also consulted widely in your department and have all of the appropriate permissions*

Informed Consent

Consent is not really enough. You are expected to give people information as to what they are agreeing to participate in, in as much detail as possible. Ideally, you should provide potential participants with an information sheet, and you should obtain written consent, which you should witness by means of a countersignature.

If you are working with children, then parental, or *in loco parentis* consent, where applicable, must be obtained. The same would apply in the case of people who are unable to give consent because of mental illness or learning disability, for example.

Undue Pressure

You must not put pressure on people to participate in your study. This includes even the mildest forms of persuasion. If someone declines to participate, you should not even say something like "Aww...please...go on...it'll only take a few minutes." Neither should you react impolitely to people who decline to participate in a rude fashion. If someone swears at you when you ask them to participate, just tell them that you are sorry to have bothered them and thank them for their time. Do not get into an argument with them, no matter what they say to you.

Deception

Sometimes no deception of the participants is necessary. If it *is* necessary due to the nature of the project, you should aim to keep the deception to a minimum, and you should explain the deception fully in the debrief. Not all deceptions are acceptable. There should be no foreseeable harm to participants leading from the deception, and you should aim to identify the likely outcomes of the 'temporary lie' that is involved. Imagine the likely reaction of your participants when you reveal the deception. If it is probably going to be something like "Oh...I see.... That's interesting" then all should be well. If you conceivably expect any participants to be offended, or to feel cheated, or you have any reason to believe that your deception may lead to bringing psychology (or your university) into disrepute, then you must think about ways to completely avoid this situation. You should not proceed where there is any possibility that you will offend participants, or create distrust or ill feeling.

Protection of Participants from Harm and 'Acceptable' Risk

You should take every precaution to prevent any of your participants being subjected to harm, whether physical or psychological. Generally, the rule of thumb to follow in determining if your project is allowable is this: you should not do anything which would put your participants at greater risk from harm than they would normally be at in their everyday lives.

Incentives

It is acceptable to provide incentives for people to participate in your research, which could take the form of a payment or a voucher, or a course credit, if your department operates such a scheme. However, you must never use an incentive to encourage participants to put themselves at risk in any way. This guidance is there to prevent poorer people from being coaxed into participation just because they need the money.

Withdrawal

You should ensure that a participant can withdraw from the investigation any time they wish, and that data which they have provided can also be removed upon request. If an individual's data cannot be identified after the collection process then you should explain this at the outset.

Confidentiality

You are under a legal obligation to protect the identities of your participants and to keep their data and/or personal details confidential. In practice, I would advise you never to ask for participants' names and other details unless you absolutely must, such as in cases where you need to contact them to arrange follow-up sessions. If you don't have the information, you don't need to worry about keeping it confidential. Note that anonymity does not always guarantee confidentiality. Imagine where you have collected data from other students in your year. You have taken personal details, but not names. If you have a participant who is the only 48-year-old male on your course, or the only black female, or the only disabled person, those people could be identified by someone else quite easily. In such cases, you still need to be careful about protecting identities of participants.

Debriefing

An important part of the research process is the debriefing of participants. This is especially the case when some kind of mild deception is involved. One way to save time and to maximise the impact of the debriefing is to present a 'debriefing sheet' at the end, rather than explain everything over and over again to each participant. If you do this, however, make sure that there is some form of contact number or email address available so that a person who has questions after reading their sheet can find you to ask them.

Never force a debrief on a participant. Sometimes people really don't care why you are doing what you are doing. They are quite willing to take part, but then want to dash off. If they don't want to be debriefed, it is their choice. However, use of a debriefing sheet also gets around this problem because they can take it away to read at their leisure.

Personal Safety

One note of caution is necessary. Never give your address to participants, nor your home telephone number. Don't use a work email address. In short, do not give personal details which could allow a participant to trace you. A mobile telephone number is generally safe, and if you want to give an email address, set up an email account with an established internet source. The best advice is to use your university department as a contact for you, provided that your supervisor agrees to this. Furthermore, do not meet potential participants in any place where you do not feel safe. If you are conducting work outside the laboratory, use public places where possible, and ensure that your mobile telephone is turned on (but with the ringer turned off so as not to disturb your interview or test situation). Make sure also that a friend or family member knows where you are. Although you are extremely unlikely to encounter any problems, one can never rule out danger, even when you are acquainted with the people you are dealing with.

⊞ OBTAINING ETHICAL CLEARANCE

In all departments there will be some system of ethical clearance for student projects. You will be expected to gain approval before you can proceed. This system can vary considerably, from obtaining approval from your supervisor, to having all projects cleared by an ethics committee. Your department will advise on what you must do to satisfy any local conditions placed upon research at your university. Usually some paperwork will be necessary. Make sure that you fill in all forms carefully, and that any committee is given full information in order to make a decision. Note also that if you change your project for any reason, whether practical or otherwise, you will normally have to submit a new proposal for ethical clearance.

Sometimes, you will also have to obtain external ethical clearance, for example when you are intending to obtain access to patients in a hospital environment. Again, your supervisor will work with you to achieve this, but you must plan well in advance should this be necessary. Ethics committees attached to hospitals and the like sometimes only meet every few months. The paperwork usually has to be distributed to members of the committee a few weeks before they convene. This will often have to include copies of any questionnaires you might be using. If you are unlucky enough to have to wait a while until a meeting occurs, and your project is rejected because more information is needed, or things need to be modified, you might then have to resubmit to another future meeting. You can lose the whole of the time allotted to working on your project in this way. This is not intended to put you off proceeding with a good project which involves hospitals, clinics or schools, but to alert you to the fact that you must start very early indeed if you are relying upon an external committee to assess your research.

One of the main concerns of external ethics committees is that the work you are conducting is not just being done to help you to achieve a degree. In the case of hospital-related ethics committees, their job is to protect patients from fatigue, anxiety, and the like. Hospitals are not there to help you to conduct your research. In particular, you will not be allowed to conduct a project unless you can clearly demonstrate that your work will either have direct benefit to the patients taking part, or to future patients. It can be indirect, through the creation of useful knowledge, but there must be some obvious benefit which you should be spelling out clearly in your ethics forms. Research for research's sake is not allowable.

You will, if you are working with 'vulnerable' groups, such as children, be expected to obtain clearance from the appropriate authorities. To protect these groups, a check on your personal circumstances (principally whether or not you have a police record in respect of certain types of criminal activities) is necessary. Your department will advise on this.

✄ GETTING STARTED

When the planning is over, the fun starts. The research process *can* be fun, believe it or not, especially when you are finding something out that really interests you. Furthermore, psychology is about people. Therefore, conducting psychological research projects puts you into contact with people, and opens your eyes to the ways in which people think and behave. You meet people, and you learn about yourself. Part of studying to achieve a degree is about personal development, and nothing contributes to your personal development more than research. After all, research is a truly natural process which you have been engaging in implicitly since you were born. You live life constantly making theories about things, testing them out, and changing your theories in the light of evidence. Therefore, conducting research projects in psychology can be seen as just one more way in which you learn about how the world works and how you, as part of the world, contribute to that.

DOING RESEARCH: COLLECTING DATA

Once you have planned your research, created your materials and instructions, and obtained ethical approval, you are ready to begin the process of gathering data. In many ways, of course, this is the most important stage, since without data you have no study to report at all. It is also fraught with difficulties, because you are now dealing with the unexpected. What I mean by the unexpected is 'people'. One of the reasons that you are studying psychology is probably that you find people interesting, at least one would hope so. Sometimes people are very predictable, but at other times they are far from that. Collecting data normally involves dealing with people, and you can often learn a lot more about them from this process than you do from the theories you might study throughout your course. Your job, as an interviewer, data collector or experimenter, is to get the most and the best out of your participants whilst ensuring that they enjoy their experience and leave you happy and feeling like they have made a contribution for which you are grateful. Collecting data can really put your interpersonal skills to the test (but the positive side of this is that you can use this experience as a selling point when applying for jobs).

♯ STUDENT–SUPERVISOR RELATIONS

Getting on with your supervisor is normally easy, of course. The roles are well defined, and most people are quite skilled at working with each other within this context. However, things can go wrong, and most supervisors will have known of cases where a student and supervisor simply did not get along. As psychologists we should be accepting of the fact that personality clashes can and do occur. They do not mean that one person is right and another wrong, but simply that two people can often see things in different ways which cannot be merged or reconciled.

All departments have some formal or informal way of dealing with such clashes between student and supervisor, and although they are sometimes difficult to work out in practice without hurt to feelings somewhere along the line. The usual pattern for working out these issues is for the student to approach the person responsible for overseeing projects and explain what the problem is. Occasionally, this will be a problem in itself, for example where the project leader is also the personal supervisor. In such cases, students are often advised to see the 'course administrator' or 'course leader'.

The most common reason for seeking another supervisor is where the student feels that the supervisor won't let them do what they want to do. Both a good and a bad supervisor can be accused of this. As a student you have a responsibility to listen to the advice of your supervisor. A good supervisor might tell you that you can't do what you want to do because it is impractical or downright impossible. A bad supervisor might, however, also push you away from what you want to do because they are simply not interested in it or regard it as a dead topic based only on personal preferences. Before you seek to change supervisor, make sure you know why your supervisor is suggesting a different research topic.

Once you know what the problem is, seek out help as soon as possible. Most of the time the problem can be sorted out without a change of supervisor being necessary. However, in the words of Judith Bell (1999, p. 31), "if all efforts to improve the position fail, then the only thing to do is to request a change before depression and a feeling of hopelessness take over."

Bell also suggests that an essential part of the research supervision process can be keeping records of the supervision, and indeed many departments have such a system. Students are often assigned a set number of hours of supervision, and I have always kept a record of this because it is useful to both supervisor and student. I have a log which students sign at the end of each session. Should a student have a complaint, which thankfully has never happened to me, the log provides evidence of the amount of time spent with the supervisor and what was discussed at each stage. If a student were to say that they had not been able to see me enough and had been deprived of supervision, I could show that they had signed for their time and that the record demonstrated that the required number of hours had been given. However, if I was genuinely remiss, I would not have the student signatures. I could not prove that I had properly supervised the student, and they would have a strong case against me. Therefore, this is a way of protecting both parties against abuse of the system.

If all is well, your supervisor will usually spend a reasonable share of your allotted time with you at the start of the project, making sure that you are prepared. This often includes ensuring that you have conducted a pilot study to get a good sense of whether the research will actually work.

⊞ PILOT STUDIES

There is always a small group of students who fail to undertake a pilot study. By doing so they can miss some important problems in their research which only reveal themselves when it is too late. However, not all students who do conduct pilot studies make the most of them, in my experience. The best pilot studies should always include the opportunity for participants to feed back their thoughts to the researchers. If you simply use a pilot study to run through the instructions, and so on, and to make sure that participants seem to be doing the right things, you are relying only on your perception of the events. There are two sides to every story.

- If you are conducting pilot interviews, ask your participants to comment on the interview afterwards. See if they found any issues difficult to talk about, or any questions hard to comprehend, or if they feel that there are other things they would have liked to mention.
- If you are conducting a pilot experimental study involving some kind of memory or perceptual activity, possibly involving computer presentations of stimuli, ask the participants to comment on what they were thinking as they took part, and any strategies that they might have used to help them. You could discover that people were actually doing something in their heads which completely changes your interpretation of the data.
- If you are conducting a questionnaire pilot, make sure that you give the participants the opportunity to ask questions about your questions. Just because you think something is clear doesn't mean that it is.
- In the case of observational studies, a pilot study will tell you exactly how observable the behaviour you are interested in actually is. Sometimes you will find that you will need forty eyes and a dozen hands to keep track of what you intend to research. You might need to adapt your study to overcome a number of practical obstacles.

DON'T BOOK THIS ROOM ON
FRIDAY THE 13TH OR APRIL 1ST

♯ DEALING WITH PEOPLE

It is likely that a great many, if not all, of your participants will be students. A lot of undergraduate research makes use of the fact that there are thousands of students milling around campuses and who tend to be quite willing to participate. Of course, you are generally encouraged to try to spread your sample out more widely, since students are usually of a restricted age range and are not necessarily always typical of the larger population. Whilst students differ in their personalities, educational history, life experiences, and so on, they are certainly not as diverse as the general population. Now and then researchers can be surprised at how the general public typically behave, especially when taking part in research, and you too should be prepared for all eventualities when you are engaging in research with human beings. Most books on the research process will skim over the problems that you can face in the interpersonal issues that can arise in psychological research, or instead they focus on some of the more theoretical aspects, such as the fact that you must produce standardised instructions in order to create a level playing-field for all participants, and that you should treat all persons fairly, respectfully and equally. There is, however, much more to the process of working with people than that. Your interpersonal skills really can be put to the test quite significantly.

Being an Ambassador

You must never forget that when you are researching, you effectively are an ambassador. Some might say that 'diplomat' is a more fitting word, since you certainly need to be diplomatic. You must be aware that, to some extent, people may see you as an example of a number of categories of people. Anything other than perfect behaviour can bring a lot of others into disrepute. This is quite a weight to carry on your shoulders, but carry it you must. You are representing the subject of psychology as a whole, but you are also in some ways representing your university or college, and students in general.

Psychology has a rather mixed reputation when it comes to the general public. On the one hand, people commonly think that psychologists have all sorts of insights into human behaviour, which usually they don't. People often think that you can read their minds. Similarly, they believe that you can analyse them in some way. They may think that psychology is synonymous with clinical psychology, or equally commonly, psychiatry. On the other hand, some members of the public have a view of psychologists as being quite useless. They might base this on their opinions of some of the more trivial ways in which psychologists are represented on television, where an expert guest on a television or radio show might not really have the opportunity to say anything particularly profound or insightful. Sometimes psychologists say things which are very obvious to the casual observer, and anyone who seems to be paid to say the obvious does not endear themselves to the public. Of course, a lot of psychology is obvious and a lot isn't, and just because something is obvious does not mean that it is not worth pointing out. However, some people hold a negative image of psychologists, and you should be aware of this. It is one of the reasons, perhaps, why some people refuse to take part in our research. They might feel that it is not worth contributing to. Equally, those people who are concerned that psychologists are mind-readers or able to 'read' body language may also refuse to participate because of a fear that they will be somehow 'exposed'. It is not your job to try to correct the public misperceptions of psychology single-handedly, but the way that you conduct yourself as a student of psychology can certainly influence those notions.

You should present yourself to participants as a *student* of psychology, making this very clear. Under no circumstances should you refer to yourself as a psychologist, nor should you engage with a discussion of people's problems in life or offer advice on things. You can politely explain to people that you aren't qualified to help them or to comment on the things that they might tell you or want answers for. Whether a participant is utterly serious or quite jocular when they ask you questions, you should always refrain from offering advice or help.

Having said this, one aspect of being an ambassador for psychology is to be well prepared, in terms of knowledge. You must be ready to answer questions about your study, and its theoretical basis, should participants ask. Prepare a little speech in answer to the common questions which participants might ask you. Make sure that you have a simple explanation prepared, rather than a complicated one which only students of psychology would understand. The questions you can expect to be asked are:

- What is the theory behind this research?
- What's the point of this?
- What will this tell you that we don't already know?
- What does this tell you about *me*?

Looking ignorant of what you are actually doing is a very embarrassing situation. Not only do you end up with egg on your face, you also flick it on to others' faces too.

In my experience of psychology over the years, I have found myself in a number of situations which needed a good deal of tact and care, and I have also heard a great many stories about the behaviour of participants which have made me think hard about human behaviour. Just to give you a sense of what you may sometimes have to deal with, here are some true examples. Bear in mind that such things are rare.

- One participant tried to pass on racist literature to the researcher, and to gain support for their right-wing views from him.
- One participant was very critical of psychology, and became agitated at some aspects of the research. In taking part in a study which involved naming colours, he claimed that he disliked colours because 'they were for women', and thumped the laptop computer in front of him when asserting his opinions, thus putting expensive equipment in jeopardy. He also claimed that he had been given a pen which was moving as he tried to write.
- Another participant, a sailor, actually bit the arm of the researcher, albeit playfully.
- During a session of tasks which involved putting letters and numbers in order, it became clear that the participant did not know the alphabet, and was confused by the most basic of mathematical operations. This meant that the person would not have been able to take part in the research fully. The researcher had to hastily find a way to terminate the research early, whilst still helping the participant to maintain their dignity and feel they had contributed.

These examples are presented not as interesting or amusing anecdotes, but in a serious context to make you think about what your reactions would be in these and other, similar, situations.

Working with Participants

Participants are people. In fact, they are people one hundred per cent of the time, and participants for only a very tiny fraction of their lives. You should never forget that. You should also never forget that they are giving up some of their lives to help you, even if only for a few minutes. They deserve your respect, even if you don't particularly agree with them, or understand their way of life, or if you personally find them less than amiable individuals. Here we can deal with some of the common types of participants that you may encounter, and how you should deal with them and your natural reactions to them.

Shy and quiet participants

This is mainly a problem for interview studies, where you really need people to be as forthcoming as possible. Principally, you should remember that people are quite entitled to be shy or unforthcoming, as befits them. It is your responsibility to try to find ways to encourage them to talk, whilst never trying to pry into things which they do not want to talk about. Sometimes people do not answer questions fully because they have not understood them. You need to be flexible in your approach, and be able and willing to venture paraphrases of your questions if you feel that someone has not explored a topic fully. You will get the most out of your interviewees if you have made it very clear, from the start, that you are not looking for particular answers to questions, and that you are genuinely interested in their own opinions on the subjects being raised. You can do this during the interview, too, by using the right words in your discourse. Ask questions like "What do you feel about that?", "What is your opinion about...?", "What do you make of...?", "What do you think about...?"

Often, quiet participants need 'warming up' to the interview situation. This may affect many people who are being interviewed on emotive topics. Most of you are familiar with the kind of difficult conversation, perhaps between friends or partners or family members, which goes like this:

'Is there something wrong?'
'No, nothing. I'm fine.'
'You sure?'
'Yes.'
'I'm not convinced. I know you and I think something's wrong.'
'No, honestly, I'm just tired.'
'Well, if you say so, but if there's anything bothering you I'd prefer that you told me.'
'How many times do I have to tell you that I'm fine?'
'It's just that you are not yourself....'
'I'm okay, I'm just...'
'What?'
'Nothing.'
'What?'
'Well, if you really want to know...'

Now, obviously, you shouldn't conduct an interview like this. The point here, however, is that you can see what 'warming up' can mean. If you have ever wondered why conversations often go like this, it is because you can't just launch into talking about sensitive, difficult or personal issues from cold. Therefore, try to get your interviewee talking about something, anything at all, and work your way into the key issues.

Occasionally, you might want to question someone's opinion in order to explore their ideas fully. You don't want to come across as if you are suggesting that their opinion is somehow wrong, so you must do this carefully. A common technique (listen to interviewers on the TV and radio and you'll see this), is to distance the challenge by putting it into the mouth of a third party. Let's imagine that someone says that they think that there is no realistic opposition to the government. You might explore this further by saying 'Some people would say that there could be a realistic opposition if voters would consider some of the smaller parties who traditionally don't get much support. What would you say to them?' Note that this is not presented as your opinion, but a discussion point about what others might believe. Be careful though; depending upon the nature of your methodological approach to interviewing, such questions might be ruled out altogether. Be sensitive to the theoretical dimensions to your research. Speak to your supervisor about this situation before you mentally prepare for such an eventuality.

You must be willing to allow an interview to reach its natural conclusion. Never push your interviewees into saying more than they want to. If someone is not very talkative, accept that, and be just as polite to them as you would a person who has provided you with particularly rich data. You might not be able to use their transcript because it doesn't really contain anything to analyse. That is your problem, not theirs, and they should leave you feeling that you are happy with their contribution, and grateful for it too.

Aggressive and argumentative participants

Never get into an argument with a participant, even when they are trying their best to create one. Remain calm and allow them to have their say. Be professional and confident, but not arrogant. Many people who naturally seek debate and argument will give up if they find that you are not willing to play the game. Be aware that sometimes genuinely enthusiastic people can seem aggressive or argumentative even when they are not. So can nervous or anxious people. Don't assume the worst of people: rather, assume the best. Often, people are looking for a discussion of the issues around your research rather than a heated debate.

It is not uncommon for participants to suggest that you ought to do your research differently, because they have different ideas. Listen to them. Sometimes they actually have a great idea which you would be foolish not to take on board. On the other hand, they also might be suggesting something which is much less sensible. Rather than enter into a complicated debate about why you think they are wrong, you are best advised to

" PLEASE TAKE PART,
OR I'LL HAVE TO SHOUT
AT SOME PUPPIES! "

treat their suggestion with respect and to tell them that you will certainly take their comments into account and consider their ideas. You are not lying. Even an idea that you will dismiss in seconds needs to be considered in order to throw it out.

Politically incorrect participants

Now and then, participants might say things in a politically incorrect way which actually offends you to some degree. Here you must rely on your judgement as to the appropriate way to respond. You must balance the need to be polite and accepting of others with your principles. At times, you may just choose to ignore the comments, and at others you might want to deflect them with a phrase such as 'I can see why you might think that.' Such a statement does not at all mean that you agree with what the person is saying. Another useful phrase is 'I understand what you are saying.' You retain your dignity, whilst avoiding a difficult situation. Note that you are not under any obligation, however, to accept any language or behaviour which you find to be very offensive. If you ever find yourself in a situation where you cannot simply 'grin and bear it', you should firmly and politely explain that you do not share your participant's opinions. Equally, as a human being you have a right not to be subjected to abuse. Hopefully, however, such an experience will never present itself.

Talkative participants

When a person volunteers to help you with your research, they might do so for a variety of reasons. Some people are keen to learn about what you are doing. Some are looking for confirmation about their hypotheses concerning what psychologists get up to. Others want someone to listen to their ideas. Some people want to talk. Always remember that your participant has given up some of their time for you, and so you should be willing to give up your time for them too. This doesn't mean that you must become their best friend, which would be unprofessional, but you should take an interest in what they have to say and let them talk if they wish to. If someone wants to talk during the research itself, you can politely explain to them that you will be very happy to chat with them at the end but that it's important that they concentrate only on the task while they are doing it. Most people will respond very favourably to that kind of approach as long as you are polite. If someone really will not leave your laboratory or other research setting because they are particularly talkative, then you may have to explain to them that you have another appointment. It is always easier to accept that someone is not *able* to talk to you any more than to live with the feeling that they don't *want* to.

Anxious participants

Some participants are particularly anxious with respect to engaging with your research. Sometimes this is because they are anxious about most things, that is, if they are that kind of person. Others are willing to take part but are just worried about how they will perform in your tasks. Always reassure people, and *never* refer to anything you do as a 'test'. The word 'test' instantly conjures up images of schooldays, and of being assessed or measured in some way, and often of being compared with other people. I always get around this by using the term 'task', which is much more neutral.

It is normally the case that, in experimental studies at least, you are not actually interested in individual performances but rather the average scores obtained by groups of people. Make sure that your participants are aware of this should they express any views that they are worried about being 'tested' in any way.

Children

Children present some specific problems. As an adult, they might look up to you and expect to learn from you. You should never contradict anything that their parents or teachers have told them. It is not your role to do this. If a child misbehaves you should try to bring them back to the task in hand, but should never shout at them or raise your voice at all. Treat them as if they were adults, relying on the content of what you are saying to persuade them to concentrate on the task at hand, not the volume of your speech. If a child really will not concentrate, it is occasionally necessary to terminate the research session prematurely. If this is done carefully the child will not notice this. Generally, you should interpret a child's lack of engagement with or interest in a task as an implicit withdrawal of their consent (something recommended by the British Psychological Society).

For legal reasons, some people might actually advise you not to conduct research with children unless there is someone else present. You may even find that some schools also insist on this as a matter of course. Do not be offended if they suggest this to you. They are not only protecting the children from potential difficulties, but are also, in effect, guarding you too, against any false accusations of mistreatment which could arise. Whilst this is very rare at present, one can certainly envisage such practices becoming common as parents and teachers become increasingly concerned about keeping children safe from harm. Be aware that, in the UK, it is necessary for you to be checked against police records before you are allowed into schools. This is not only a good precaution which you should not be offended by, but something which does take time, so be ready for any delays in this process which could hold your project back.

When Participants Don't Understand or Make Mistakes

You can never quite predict the ways in which a participant might misinterpret your instructions. Even the seemingly clearest directions can fox some people. If people simply do not understand what you are asking them to do, try to explain in a different way. You will have broken your rules of engagement, as it were, because your standardised instructions will go out of the window, but you don't have to use the data. As long as your participant gets no sense of the fact that you cannot use their data then their feelings are not hurt. Some might argue that this is a form of deception, but it is more important to protect the participant from harm than it is to tell the truth and make them feel unworthy of your research.

Often your participants will make mistakes and be very aware of doing so. Some can laugh this off, whereas others will feel ashamed and even stupid. Never allow a participant to feel this way without attempting to reassure them. Learn to respond like the researcher does in the following examples:

PARTICIPANT: I just can't do this. It's really hard.
RESEARCHER: Some people do find this very difficult. Please don't worry.
PARTICIPANT: I'm no good at this. I bet I'm the worst you've seen.
RESEARCHER: Different people are good at different things, but I think that this is quite a difficult task. I will be looking at the data I get from groups of people, so I shan't compare any individual scores with any others.
PARTICIPANT: I don't understand what I have to do.
RESEARCHER: I'm sorry. I don't think I have explained this to you very well. I'll go through it again.

Never allow a situation to develop where a participant leaves you feeling like they have done badly. Always explain that there is no such thing as 'badly', and that you are simply interested in *how* people do things, not how *well* they do them. If a person is becoming very upset because of their performance, you should consider terminating the research session early.

However, if you do this you should aim to finish things at a point where the person feels like things have come to an end, and you should not let them know that you have taken the decision to cut things short. Again, the feelings of the participants are far more important than some abstract 'truth' about the nature of their participation.

⊞ CONDUCTING INTERVIEWS: THE PRACTICALITIES

Make sure that you minimise the possibility that the machinery you are using will fail. Use a mains-operated tape recorder if possible, but have batteries in it too, so that you can switch to battery power should a fuse blow or there be a power cut. Don't run out of tape. Carry spares. Make sure that the microphone works before you start. You should also ensure that you have written consent from the participant for the session to be recorded.

If you have booked a room for the purposes of interviewing, make sure that you overbook, so that you have a little more time than you think that you need. You will be annoyed, frustrated and embarrassed if you have to terminate an interview because someone else has booked the room and you are over-running. You will also find that you might have to scrap that particular interview, meaning that you waste time and effort.

Make sure that you have a notice on the door informing people that they are not to disturb you. You have an obligation to your interviewees to make sure that you are not disturbed, since someone popping their head around the door might compromise anonymity and confidentiality, in addition to creating anxiety and leaving you looking ill prepared.

⊞ OBSERVATIONAL STUDIES

If your study is an observational one, there are a number of practical issues to consider and keep in mind as you go along. You need to make sure that you have all the materials you need before you start the observation. This is especially important where the observations are *in vivo*, that is where you are noting down what happens in real life as it happens, rather than watching a video recording of the behaviours in question. It might sound obvious, but make sure that you have a spare pen, for example!

If you are making non-intrusive observations, make sure that they are. For lots of reasons, don't sit around with a clipboard and pen staring at people and making notes. If you do, it is only a matter of time before someone wants to know what you are doing, and not everyone will be happy when you explain.

Ensure that you have a very clear coding scheme and have piloted it first. It's too late if you start your study only to find that the behaviours you are looking for happen too quickly and furiously for you to actually keep track of them. The more things you are looking for, the greater the possibility that you will miss some of them as you are looking down and scribbling on a piece of paper.

Keep your eye not only on the behaviours you are interested in, but also on the context in which they occur. Sometimes, you can't make sense of what is happening, or not happening, unless you know what else is going on. The context can explain everything. Imagine you are intending to observe aggressive gestures made by men and women in conversation. You spot two young people on a park bench and sit some distance away. You notice that the man is waving his arms around, and they seem to be arguing. You are busy 'clocking' all of these 'data', but you notice that they come and go in waves. One minute they seem to be chatting normally, then they argue again. After a few cycles of this behaviour you notice that the aggressive behaviour seems to repeat itself almost perfectly. Each time there is a calm period between the aggression. Then you work it out. They are drama students practising a scene for a new play. You scrap everything, and head off to look for some 'real' behaviour. Of course, if you didn't work out what was happening....

If you are observing out and about, you must not do this without permission, where appropriate. Always check with your supervisor as to suitable places to make observations, and don't stray from the agreed observation points without seeking advice.

RELYING ON EQUIPMENT

Research often involves relying on equipment, most commonly computers. Of course, equipment is wonderful until it malfunctions, when suddenly it becomes the object of your anger and hatred! If you are using equipment for research, try to have plans for what would happen when it goes wrong. Make sure that the equipment carries a current safety certificate, where appropriate. Usually your university will ensure this, but check in case something has slipped through the net.

One problem that you might have to deal with is where a computer crashes, possibly losing some data. When this happens, your natural reaction might be to swear, be angry, or show your despair. Don't. You have a responsibility to your participant to remain calm and professional. If you make a fuss, or show anger, there is a possibility that the participant might take this personally. They might think that they have 'broken' the equipment, and that they are at fault. By reacting calmly, you can convey to them that the technical difficulty is not their fault, and that it is not really a big problem at all, *even if it is.*

♯ MAKING BACKUPS

As soon as is physically possible, back up all of your data. Make copies of all computer files which you will need for the purposes of analysis, and make sure that those copies are stored somewhere safe. Your back-ups must be stored so that the confidentiality of your participants is just as protected as is it in your original data files.

Floppy disks can be easily corrupted, so buy a disk holder for them, rather than have them loosely stored in your bag, able to be affected by dust or damage to the spring-loaded metal catch that protects the disk's surface. Furthermore, don't leave a disk somewhere where it can be affected by moisture, heat or a magnetic field. Keep disks away from your computer monitor, and away from any speakers. Also, don't leave disks in sunlight, or in a car, where higher temperatures can destroy what is contained in them. In addition, storing disks anywhere near your mobile telephone is best avoided.

Today, recordable CDs are becoming more and more commonplace. Whilst they are not incorruptible, they are generally more robust than floppy disks and so you should use them for backing up data wherever possible.

♯ ADJUSTING YOUR PROJECT MILESTONES

As your project progresses, do not be afraid to adjust your project milestones, i.e. your timetable can be changed to take into account unplanned-for events and either unusually fast or unusually slow work on your behalf. Create a new Gantt chart, as appropriate, and discuss this with your supervisor. In fact, I have hardly ever seen a research project which progressed in accordance with the original estimates of either time or cost. Of course, it's not only researchers who plan things wrongly. Most of us are familiar with the builder or other contractor who takes an inordinate amount of time to finish a job which they originally said would be completed in two weeks!

⌗ TAKING PART YOURSELF

One of the most educating of experiences that you can have as a psychologist is taking part in other people's studies. When you are busy with your own research it can be difficult to find time to participate in the research of your peers or your lecturers, but you ought to try to involve yourself if possible. Far too often, psychologists spend their days engaged in the role of experimenter or interviewer. However, if you really want to know what participants think and feel, you should try being one regularly yourself. Things may occur to you about your own research, too. You are very

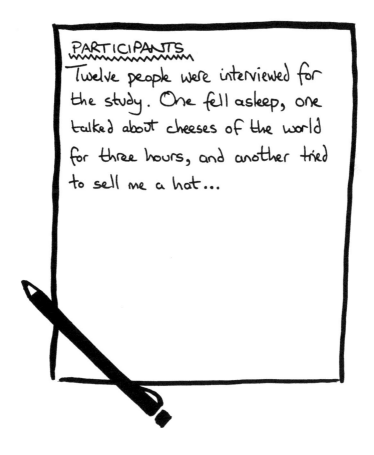

familiar with the inside of your own home. Try stepping outside and looking at the exterior. Look carefully, and you will start to see things you were not aware of, like ill-fitting bricks, or water stains, or misplaced roof-tiles, or even a door or window which is slightly askew. So it is with research. When you take the role of 'the man or woman in the street', you will be surprised what you learn.

♯ REVISITING DATA

This is mainly an issue for qualitative work, where sometimes you must generate theories as you go along, and then further test those theories by going back to interviewees, conducting further interviews, and so on. This back-and-forth motion is what characterises well-conducted grounded theory research, for instance.

One practical problem can occur here, in that you might have trouble going back and conducting more interviews unless you have sown the seeds of this with your interviewees. If you know that you are likely to have to re-interview, make sure that you have contact details for your interviewees, and that you have informed them, from the start, that you might want to talk to them again in the near future.

♯ TRANSCRIBING INTERVIEWS

If you are conducting interviews and tape recording them, you will need to transcribe them. This means taking the recorded speech and converting it to a set of written documents which can then be read by others and quoted from in your write-up. I have included this in the 'Doing' chapter of this book because you ought to be transcribing interviews as you go along, as soon as possible after each interview. There are two reasons for this. First, transcribing takes a long time. Second, if you transcribe while you still remember what was said during the interview you will be able to interpret any utterances which have not clearly recorded on to the tape. If you wait until much later, you might have forgotten what was being said when all you can hear is "umph...gr...at...ping... nolly...et...sems"!

Do not underestimate the amount of time it will take you to transcribe your interviews. No matter what kind of transcription you employ, it will always take ages to type up even the shortest interviews. Generally, expect a one-hour interview to take anything up to twenty hours to transcribe properly, even if you can type very rapidly. If you are a little clumsy with a keyboard, then give yourself even more time.

Transcription schemes vary massively, and your tutor will advise on the best method of transcription for your particular purpose. The most simple is to transcribe only the words, in the form of normal English, ignoring anything which isn't a word. Of course, this would rarely be a useful form of transcription, since most of the time you can learn a great deal from the other aspects of speech, often called 'non-verbal utterances'. These can include coughing, laughing, stuttering, and filler noises such as 'um', 'er', 'erm', 'urgh' and 'ahh'. Listen to anyone talking, and you will find hundreds of these in just a few minutes of speech. The more emotive the subject being discussed, the more of these you will generally find.

You might also want to make sure that you include pauses, and changes in tone or volume of speech. Sarcasm cannot be conveyed in a straightforward transcription, for example. However, you shouldn't fail to take notice of a sarcastic tone, because it can change the whole nature of what is being said. Equally, there are many ways to say the word 'yes'. Try it. You'll probably find that you can say it in around a dozen different ways, each conveying something different. The most common could be the yes that means no, the orgasmic yes, the sarcastic yes, the incredulous yes, the angry yes, the bored yes, the yes of agreement, and so on.

The point I am making is that the more you take these things into account, the longer it takes to transcribe. You will need to go over the tape again and again and again. Each time you can add more and more detail until you have completed the transcript. The first two or three passes of the tape will be taken up in typing the main body of what is being said. Once you have done this, you can start to add greater and greater detail. Rather than trying to add pauses and non-verbal utterances and tones to the transcript all at once, make a pass through the transcript to add pauses, and then turn to other utterances in a separate pass. Take another pass to add tones, and so on until the transcript is finished. Hopefully you can now see why you need to plan a lot of time for this activity.

THE PAPER TRAIL

In qualitative work, keeping a paper trail is generally seen as essential. You need to be able to trace all of your ideas. Keep files carefully, and keep a research diary so that you do not only have a record of your ideas but a record of the history of your ideas as well, in chronological order. However, those of you conducting quantitative work should also consider keeping a diary. Furthermore, you should carry it with you so that you can write down ideas as they occur to you. In my own experience, my best ideas do not come when I sit down with a cup of tea and try to think hard about something. Instead, they fly at me out of nowhere and hit me in the face at inconvenient moments, like during a meeting, or when in the shower, or out shopping. I now keep a small notebook with me just in case (although I don't take it into the shower).

⌗ KNOWING WHEN TO STOP

As the data collection starts drawing to a close, you have to be firm with yourself about when to actually shut the computer down, or when to stop photocopying questionnaires. Research becomes addictive, especially if you have a bit of a compulsive character. However, you have limited time, and those 'last few participants' for good measure can take a long time to secure. When you have collected the data that you intended to collect, stop there.

You still have a long way to go. You might have transcription to finish, or a whole set of printed material to wade through, carefully marking answers and totting up numbers. This will take time to do properly.

⌗ DATA PREPARATION

When you start adding up responses and typing them into your statistics database, remember that a few simple mistakes in this process can mean that any subsequent analysis is reduced to nonsense. You'd be a fool to type in your data and go ahead with an analysis without checking and double-checking. Furthermore, ideally you should ask someone else to do the double-checking. What you miss, another person might spot, and vice versa. It is very easy to accidentally slip a finger over a key on the keyboard and type 20.0 instead of 2.0. It is a common error to type 4, 4, 5, 5, instead of 4, 4, 4, 5, and so on. Although the occasional error will probably not muck up your analysis at all, there is a chance that it could. I have known instances where students have shown me their analysis and I have looked at the means of the groups concerned and noticed that something seemed amiss. I usually ask to see the original data. Often I have seen a column of figures all under 10 except one score of 1,458. Imagine what that can do to a mean score in a list of a couple of hundred numbers! So, check your data, and get someone else to cross-check.

In a quantitative project, you will be required to 'treat' the data in some way before conducting your analysis. Raw data often contain all sorts of 'noise' which needs to be filtered out. Removing extreme scores (outliers) is not cheating. Naturally, you must mention this when you report your analyses in your Results section, but it is a common process and actually helps your data to make sense. Of course, you should consult your supervisor about this, since there might be some debate over what counts as an outlier and what does not. One quirky score in a hundred ought to be removed, but when you have quite a few very high or very low scores you should start to think if this is telling you something quite important.

⌗ CONDUCTING STATISTICAL ANALYSES

When it is time to start doing statistical analysis on your data, in the case of quantitative work, you will probably be using a statistical package such as *SPSS for Windows*. There are many books which provide excellent advice on the details of this, and it is not relevant to go into this here. However, here are a few general tips:

- Don't enter you data until you are certain that you are inputting them correctly. If in doubt, check with your lecturer beforehand. Nothing is more frustrating for both supervisor and student than finding that the data are in the wrong format to conduct the required analysis.
- I have often seen a student typing in, for example, a long column of data consisting of very small, whole numbers, then another column, and then asking their statistics package to add them up to create a third column. Then they delete the first two columns. This can take more time (and possibly be subject to more error) than simply adding the two columns up mentally and simply typing in the result. I am not suggesting you use mental arithmetic for complex calculations, but most people don't need a computer to add 6 to 3!
- Don't forget, if you are using SPSS, to save *both* your data file and your output file.
- It is easy to forget which analysis is which in an SPSS output file. If you click on the large, emboldened titles, you can edit them, thus labelling each analysis in a way which clears up any confusion. This is probably better than saving each analysis in a separate output file, because one long file takes up less disk space than a number of separate ones.
- Don't forget to make sure that you have all of the appropriate descriptive statistics to go with each inferential analysis.

- Don't conduct or interpret analyses until you are satisfied that you have met all of their assumptions. Therefore, always check for normality using a statistic like the Shapiro-Wilk, and pay attention to things like Levene's Test for Equality of Variances, sphericity, and multicollinearity.

3 WRITING UP RESEARCH

In some ways, writing up research can be very easy. It rarely seems so to the average student, but it's really a question of perspective. Writing up research is mostly governed by a set of rules, such as those set by the American Psychological Association (APA). They have generated advice on what to put where, and what to say and what not to say, which applies to almost everything you could possibly need in psychology. So in many ways, being told exactly what to do is surely easier than being in the dark? Let's try an analogy. I ask you to put my socks away for me. I tell you that the top drawer is where I keep my socks. How difficult is that? Writing a report is a bit like this. You are told what the rules are; you are advised as to what goes where. But what if I were to ask you to put my socks away without telling you where I put them? You're much more likely to get it wrong. This is like writing an essay; the rules are not so clear. So for those of you who think that essays are easier than writing up research, try to remember this.

Some of the rules governing writing-up research are arbitrary. A team of people made them up, and they really did not *have* to be that way. There were other possibilities. However, now that we have a system to work to, we'd better just get on with it. Most journals in psychology have a house style based upon APA guidelines, so if you write up research in this way you are closer to the format required for publication as well. Your particular psychology department might have its own rules as to how you should report research, but mostly they will follow the APA guidelines. Remember to do what your tutors say if it is different from what you find in this book (but it's very unlikely to be all *that* different).

It is easy to get quite confused when reading journal articles because you will encounter a wide range of formats, especially when reading older articles. Not every journal follows the APA guidelines. It's mainly up to the founders, editors and publishers of a journal as to the style they wish to adopt. Sometimes you will find research written up without any of the standard sections. Sometimes there is no Abstract, at other times the Results and Discussion are fused together. Occasionally you will discover that certain articles have a Conclusions section. None of these are within the APA rules. If you are expected to write according to APA guidelines, don't try to emulate non-APA journal styles. Just because you see something in print, it does not mean that it is all right for you to follow that template. This is also important in writing Reference sections, where there are a great many systems in existence, and again these vary considerably across psychology journals, and even more noticeably across disciplines. Reading a piece in a sociology or politics journal can confuse you even further. If you have been asked to follow APA style, follow it. If you are required, by your department, to use some other system (such as Harvard), you will probably be told exactly what to do, and again you should ignore what you see in other journals and books.

⌗ AN OVERVIEW

Even though a research report is made up of sections, there is a bigger picture to consider too. Together those sections are like the chapters of a book. The overall purpose is to tell a story. Never forget that a good research report simply tells the story of what you did, why you did it, and what you found out. It might not be a thrilling, epic tale of bearded goblins resisting evil as they trek across mountains to find a magic sword, or the story of an erotic encounter leading to a steamy affair ending in double murder, but, nevertheless, the report writer is a storyteller. As a report writer, you have to assemble the information in a logical order so that people can read it and follow what happened. Don't lose the plot. Don't miss out important information. Don't waffle on about something unnecessary to the story.

⌗ NOTES ON STYLE

The overall style that you use to write a report is very important. For writing-up quantitative research, a very formal style is adopted. Please do not mistake formality for pomposity. It is quite possible to write something formally without it sounding like you are showing off. The most important point to remember is that you should avoid all mention of the first person. Therefore, instead of 'we thanked the participants' you should say 'the participants were thanked'. Another important point is that you should avoid contractions, such as 'didn't', 'shouldn't', 'isn't', and so on. Always write the full forms: 'did not', 'should not', 'is not', and so forth. (You will find contractions in this book, but this book is not intended to be formal.)

Another important point is that you must write in the past tense. A research report is an account of something which is already finished. Therefore, it does not make sense to present it in any other way than as a piece of history.

Qualitative reports do not always need to have the same level of formality, particularly in terms of writing in the first person. It is often quite acceptable, sometimes encouraged, to write up qualitative research with frequent mention of 'I'. However, just because qualitative research allows for some relaxing of the traditional rules of writing-up research does not mean that anything goes. You are still expected to write well and to avoid slang or colloquialisms, for example.

Whatever type of research you are writing up, try to use the simplest words wherever possible. There's no need to find the most complicated way of describing something. Be very careful not to use unusual or technical words you've come across in your reading unless you are certain of what they mean and how you should use them. Trying too hard can sometimes mean that you end up saying something quite ridiculous.

Of course, using simple words does not mean using slang, or informal or colloquial language. Words and phrases you should usually avoid include: 'maybe', 'perhaps', 'really', 'just', 'a lot', 'a bit', 'quite', 'nice', 'all sorts', and hundreds of others which can't be listed here. Hopefully you can see the point. Try to avoid value judgements, such as suggesting that things are wrong, or improper, or good, or particularly fascinating or exciting. The writer should generally be impartial and keep a distance from the research, even if he or she is personally fascinated by it.

⊞ A NOTE ON PLAGIARISM

Plagiarism is an increasing problem for universities, possibly because of the rise of the internet and the ease of cutting and pasting from one electronic document to another. It is becoming all too easy to 'steal' other people's words and ideas and pass them off as your own work. Put simply, plagiarism is, by definition, a form of theft, or at least a type of cheating. Taking another student's work is one form of plagiarism, whether by mutual consent or not. Taking work from a published source is also plagiarism. Some people do it deliberately, and clearly deserve to be punished for it. In some cases, student plagiarists can find themselves expelled from their courses. It is also possible to plagiarise accidentally, especially if you are not fully aware of what constitutes plagiarism. However, ignorance is usually not considered a defence. These days you often find that universities provide you with information on plagiarism, and promising not to plagiarise is commonly a part of your legal contract with a university, which you sign when you enrol.

Here's some help on how to avoid plagiarism:

- Don't copy chunks of text from a published source into your essays or reports. If you want to use someone else's words, quote them and cite your source.
- Don't pass off ideas which come from other people as yours. Again, cite your sources. The implicit assumption in a piece of work is that unless you have given a name and date to back up something you say, then you are presenting your own ideas.
- Don't make notes from books by copying out sections of text. If you come back to your notes after a few weeks, you might completely forget that you have literally copied, and convince yourself that the words are your own. Suddenly you find yourself slotting that text into your own work, and thus you could accidentally plagiarise. Instead, read something, think about it, understand it, put it away, and make some notes out of your head.
- Don't try to avoid plagiarism by copying out a piece of text and altering some of the words. Usually this still constitutes a breach of the rules. Write things in your own words. However, it is perfectly acceptable to use certain words when they are the only words to describe something. If a text you have read refers to 'lexical decision tasks', 'fragment completion paradigms' or 'photophobia', for example, don't try to paraphrase these special jargon terms. It is quite acceptable to use phrases like these without using quotation marks.

⌗ SECTION BY SECTION

Title

Students tend to fall into one of two groups when it comes to writing titles. One group are obsessive. They spend so long on worrying about getting a title right that they actually have no time left to do the rest of the report.

The other group take the opposite view. They think, 'it's only a title', and so they type up any old nonsense and never think twice about it. Both approaches are wrong. Titles *do* matter, a lot, but they don't matter more than everything. Getting titles right is not easy, and takes skill and experience. The purpose of a title is to accurately convey what a piece of research is about. Usually, titles are from 12 to 20 words long. You should aim to explain, using your title, what you did, and to whom, and what you concluded. Be as specific as possible, whilst avoiding an overly lengthy title as a result. It is not always possible to manage all of this, so you often have to make a judgement as to the key information that must be imparted.

The most important advice, regarding titles, is to read some. Look at the contents lists in copies of journals on your library shelves. Do this to get a sense of what you need to aim for. There is no substitute for reading and experiencing for yourselves.

If you are reporting an experimental type of study, where you have an independent and a dependent variable, it might help to consider how the title could contain mention of both. If you are looking for the effect of X on Y, then a title which says so can be very informative. The following are all acceptable:

- The effects of alcohol consumption on academic performance in post-graduate students.
- Relationships between personality variables and ethical concerns.
- Extroversion and aggression: is the link modulated by social support?
- An application of the Health Belief Model to uptake of dietary advice.

If you work it out, the average number of words per title above is ten. Each title, however, actually conveys a good sense of the research. Nothing is misleading. In the last case, the title requires the reader to know what the Health Belief Model actually is in order to understand the title fully, but this is not a problem. Someone who was interested in research of this type *would* understand it. That is what matters.

If you have many independent and/or dependent variables in your study, you should not list them in your title. This becomes unwieldy and makes the title far too long. Try to summarise them in some way. Therefore, age, sex, socio-economic status, level of education and income can be summarised as 'personal/demographic variables'. Introversion/extroversion, aggression, self-esteem, and friendliness can be summarised as 'personality variables'.

Things to avoid

- Don't start a title with 'An Investigation of...', or 'An Experiment to Discover...' or anything like this. It's mainly a waste of valuable words. Unless you have used some groundbreaking new technique, there's usually no need to mention the method. The first of these examples is the most common, but also the worst. After all, the reader surely knows that you are reporting an investigation of some sort. There's no reason to tell them. Imagine if all TV programmes were called 'A TV Programme About...'! What if, every time you went into a shop, the assistant walked up to you and said, "Hello. This is a shop"?

- Don't opt for the 'creative' title unless you *really* know how to pull it off with flair. It doesn't help the reader to see titles like 'Raining Cats and Dogs' or 'She Doesn't Understand Me'. They might be intriguing, but the purpose of the title of a research report is not to generate intrigue. You must convey a sense of what the study is about. You are telling a story, but a research report isn't actually a novel!

- Don't refer to something you have invented or developed and named yourself in your title. If you have created a special piece of software and called it *PPG-Dev*, for example, your title must not be 'PPG-Dev as an Educational Tool in Ten-Year-Olds'. How on earth is the reader supposed to understand that? They can't possibly have heard of PPG-Dev! Instead, describe the equipment in the title. So, a better title would be: 'The Use of Creative Writing Software as an Educational Tool in Ten-Year-Olds.'

Abstract

This should be the very last thing that you write. The reason for this is that it is a summary of your report. You can't trim a beard until you've grown one. What until you have finished the report, and then start on your abstract.

The abstract can vary in length, depending upon the size and nature of the study that has been conducted. It is sometimes very difficult to summarise a massive amount of research in a few words. In these cases, it is often acceptable for the abstract to be longer than average. On the whole, however, an abstract is somewhere between 150 and 250 words. Another way to think of the abstract is that is like a fleshing-out of the title. Take the title, and then explain each of the parts of it in more detail, adding some statement of results, and you might find you have an abstract on your hands.

The abstract needs to contain certain crucial information. Sometimes people only have access to the abstract of a published article, not the article itself. As a consequence of this, you must tell almost the whole story of your research, sparing the details. In order, here is what you should write, devoting approximately one sentence to each:

What needed to be explored and why. You point out that there is some kind of 'hole' in the research literature. So, you might have done the research because a particular theory had been applied to children, and young adults, but no one had thought to apply it to older people. That's what you say.

What you did. You summarise your method, explaining who took part, and what they actually were asked to do. Don't list dozens of variables; summarise them in the same way that you would summarise them in a title.

What you found. Give a statement of the results, without resorting to giving strings of numbers or specific statistical information. There's no need to give means or SDs unless there's something extremely unusual about them (and even then it's better to express this in words). Simply state the fact that Group A performed significantly better than Group B or that there was a significant relationship between X and Y.

What the implications of this are. Again, write a sentence which puts the research into context. Have you called a theory into question by disproving or refuting it? Have you supported a particular theory? Say so. If you have realised that your study is flawed which means that you can't take the results too seriously, make this point in appropriate language. You might also like to comment on what needs to be done next, i.e. further research, although academics would argue about the relevance of this in an abstract.

Reading real abstracts of research is the best way to learn how to write your own. If you need practice, try reading a journal article, ignoring the abstract. Then write your own abstract for that research, and compare yours to the published one. You'll soon realise what you're doing wrong.

Introduction

The Introduction is where you detail the research which has been conducted in the area you are concerned with. Conceptually, it is funnel-shaped. What do I mean by this? Well, you start generally, and become more specific as you continue. You describe the work that has been done, leading the reader by the hand, slowly seducing them into believing that the work you have done is really worthwhile and important. You do this subtly, however! Right at the end, you introduce the study you have conducted.

Think of the pitch of a good salesperson trying to get you to buy some gadget or other. They start by pointing out that life could be better. They make some general comments about hassles caused by a lack of a particular solution to the problems you face in life. Then, they drop the bombshell; they have exactly what you are looking for. Here it is!

Now, lecturers often point out to students that an introduction should begin with some general statements, and students often misinterpret this. We do not mean *very* general, simply general compared to what is coming later. So, if your study is in the area of working memory, *do not* begin with a statement like 'Memory is important to all organisms, and has been of interest to psychologists for decades.' This is *far too general*. Instead, start with a general statement about the specific aspect of memory that you are interested in. (So, that's general-specific, not general-general. Get it?) If you are reporting a study on working memory, here's how that first, general, sentence might look: 'Since Baddeley & Hitch's (1974) outlining of the concept of working memory, research in the area has been largely devoted to finding evidence for the specific memory subsystems that these authors posited.'

Do you see what makes this better? It is clearly general because it doesn't say a great deal about the area, but also clearly specific to working memory. It pays no lip service to any other theories of human memory. It is about working memory: nothing else. The first sentence of an Introduction section is mainly to direct the attention of the reader. What you are saying to the reader is 'get ready to start thinking about X'.

Slowly, you will make more and more specific points about the research which has been conducted and published in the past related to your particular work. You will, probably, need to consider the 'pros and cons' of different theories or techniques. Over the course of the Introduction, you will be explaining to the reader that there is something that needs to be discovered. Then, right at the end, you summarise the method of the research which has been conducted (*don't ever mention the results!*), and then give the hypothesis or research question, where appropriate.

We must pause here for a discussion of writing hypotheses. First, students are sometimes worried because they are predicting more than one thing and are unable to get all of them into one hypothesis. There's no need to do this. If you are predicting multiple outcomes of the research, then you can present more than one hypothesis. If you try to cram them into a single sentence, you are likely to befuddle the reader, so feel free to make each hypothesis into a sentence of its own. In many ways, an hypothesis is like a title; you should be aiming to express the effects of an IV on a DV, or to suggest a relationship between variables in the case of correlation or regression.

Most hypotheses begin in the same way, which is a safe pattern for students to follow, even though it is not the only way. That is, it is typical to begin with: 'It was hypothesised that...' or 'It was predicted that...'.

Tips for writing hypotheses

- If you are predicting a direction of difference, i.e. that one group will score better than another, then this should be clear from the hypothesis.
- Don't write half an hypothesis. If you say that 'it was predicted that participants in Condition One would remember a greater number of words from the list', you beg the question as to with whom they are being compared. If you predict greater recall in Condition One compared to Condition Two, say so.
- Don't forget that you must retain a formal style. Don't mention 'our hypothesis' or 'my hypothesis'.
- There is no hypothesis section. It's just a sentence or a paragraph at the end of the Introduction.
- Don't ever say 'The hypothesis stated that...'. This does not make sense. Hypotheses cannot state things. They are statements in themselves. Only a person can state things.
- Don't quote your own hypothesis. It should not appear in quotation marks.
- Unless you are specifically instructed to do so, don't include a null hypothesis. Not only have I never seen a journal article where the null hypothesis is presented, I have also never seen a student present the null hypothesis properly, since it is a subtle statistical concept which is frequently misunderstood.

Remember that you should always keep your eye on whether you are presenting a directional or non-directional hypothesis, which should then influence the nature of the statistical inferences you make in your Results section. A directional hypothesis is where you predict the direction of a difference, for example where you specifically state that Group A will score more highly than Group B. In a non-directional hypothesis you simply predict that there will be a difference between the scores of Group A and Group B. When you conduct analysis later, you should be sure that you are not tying up a non-directional hypothesis with a one-tailed statistical test.

At this point, you are now ready to describe the research in detail, and that's exactly what the Method section is for.

Method

The Method section is, quite simply, where you explain what you did, with or to whom, and you describe any special materials that you used. It is divided into four separate sections, which we can deal with separately.

Design

The Design section is where you outline the particular method that you have used. You name the design here. It's usually the first thing that you do. You'd be surprised how many students actually forget to name the design in the design section, which sounds quite ludicrous when you think about it! Normally, you can specify the design in a single, short sentence. Occasionally, you have conducted research where there is more than one kind of design. If that is the case, don't shy away from naming all of the designs used, but don't confuse the reader. Separate out the distinct studies in your research. (In fact, sometimes it is best to report each separate part on its own, with its own write-up. It is quite legitimate to have headings such as Experiment 1, Experiment 2, and so on.)

Experimental designs are generally easy to explain. They tend to be 'within-groups', or 'between-groups'. Sometimes they are 'factorial', where you have a number of IVs and/or DVs. When they are, you need to explain how many between-subjects factors there are and how many within-subjects factors are involved, and you should also name and number of the levels of these. Table 2 gives more details of the names of designs that you might need to report.

It's very common for student to omit the name of an IV, to explain it only in terms of its levels. This is incorrect. So, it is wrong to say: "There was one independent variable, which was whether the participants were taking part in the verbal or the numerical task." The IV is not named here. So, name the IV, which actually is 'task'. It has two levels: numerical or verbal. It's that simple. If you have trouble naming an IV, look at its levels and try to work backwards. So, if I gave one group of people an apple to eat and the other a banana, my IV would be 'fruit'. Imagine that I manipulated, in some way, the actual instructions I gave to participants. The IV might be described as 'instructional content'.

Table 2   Reporting Designs

What You Have Done	How the Design Is Reported
Two groups or conditions. Separate groups of people. A true experiment.	A between-groups design.
Two groups or conditions. The same people take part in each. A true experiment.	A within-groups design *or* repeated measures design.
A quasi-experiment. For instance, where the only IV is the sex of the participants, so you have not really manipulated the IV but simply observed it.	A quasi-experimental design.
Two or more sets of scores which you intend relating to each other in some way. Correlation.	A correlational design.
Questionnaires, from which you derive sets of scores, perhaps for analysis by means of correlation or multiple regression.	A questionnaire survey design. Sometimes you might call this a correlational survey design.
Interviews.	An interview survey design.
Observation, perhaps leading to a chi-squared analysis.	An observational design.
A complicated design, usually to be analysed by means of ANOVA, where you might have multiple IVs and DVs.	A factorial design. The number of levels of each variable can be specified by numbers. Therefore, a factorial design with three levels of one IV and four levels of another would be reported as 'a 3 X 4 factorial design'.

Make sure that you are very familiar with the difference between an independent and a dependent variable. The independent one is something that you group or manipulate in some way. The dependent variable is something that you measure. The different levels of the IV are what you are expecting to show up as effects on the DV. So, let's imagine that I was conducting a study into the effects of posture on memory. One group have to remember a set of words sitting down, the other group standing up. The DV is simple. It's the number of words recalled in the memory task. The IV is simply 'posture'. It has two levels, 'sitting' and 'standing'. So, in a design section, this is how I would report this: 'A between-subjects design was employed. There was one independent variable (posture) with two levels (sitting and standing). The dependent variable was the total number of words correctly recalled in a verbal memory task.'

THINGS TO AVOID

- Don't say anything like "The design was a between-groups design." Would you say "The apple was a red apple"? It's better to say something like "A between-groups design was employed."
- Don't forget to actually name the design.
- Don't just name the levels of the independent variable. Name the variable itself.
- Don't describe a correlation as an experiment. Never refer to anything as an experiment, unless it is a true experiment. If it isn't, refer to it as a 'study' or something similar.

Participants

This section is where you give details of the characteristics of the people who took part in your study. You must mention how many participants there were, preferably explaining how many in each group of your study, where appropriate. Usually, the sex of the participants is detailed (how many males and females), and there is often some mention of their ages, especially when they are from a restricted age group, such as schoolchildren. Never try to give information about your participants unless you are sure of it. Don't assume the ages of your participants just because you think you probably know them. For example, most undergraduates are between 18 and 21 years of age, but unless you have actually asked your participants how old they are you should not make assumptions. Basically, you end up lying in your report, because you are effectively making up data! The same, obviously goes for other variables such as sex or socio-economic status. Don't assume that because a group of participants are university students they have the same kind of background. Most of all, you must consider whether it is relevant to report the characteristics of your participants. Quite often, students mention that they involved a number of people of different ethnicities in their research. However, you should only do this if you have strong evidence that this is important for the research. Often it is not. If you have conducted a study into some cognitive variable such as working memory, you must think about how you reckon working memory might differ across ethnicities. Do you really believe that a person raised as a Sikh in the Punjab has a different working memory than a Namibian Christian? It is quite clear that there is really little or no evidence to suggest that ethnicity is important in the case of certain types of research. Of course, if you have interviewed people on their views of homosexuality in the clergy, or about their attitudes to spicy foods, then you really ought to be sensitive to the backgrounds of your participants, and thus should report these kinds of details.

Mention also how your participants were sampled/recruited into the study. Students often get this part wrong. It is common for people to misuse the term 'random sample'. Most studies conducted by students are not random samples, where each and every person has an equal chance of being selected for the study. In order to construct a random sample, you need a list of all of the people in a given population (such as a list of all pupils in a school), and you should randomly choose people from that list. In addition, you should use a random number generator or something similar to choose from the list; 'eeny-meeny-miny-mo' is not a random method. The majority of student research projects involve opportunity or convenience sampling. This is where you find people wherever is conveni-ent, and ask them to take part. They might be in your class, or they might be people waiting in a queue. If this applies to your study, do not refer to your sampling method as 'random'.

Never say something like 'Eighty participants took part in the research.' This is what is known as hyperbole. Participants *always* take part; what else can they do? There's no need to say it. Find another way to express what you mean to say.

Avoid also some rather odd-sounding explanations of the sex of the participants. If you are explaining how many males and females took part, give the numbers of each. If there are equal numbers of each, do be careful how you present this information. Do not end up saying something like 'Participants were both male and female.' By the same token, also avoid 'Participants were of both sexes.' Both such statements imply that individual participants might have been *both* male and female. Unless you have done some genetic testing, it's very unlikely that you might know about this, and even more unlikely that you will have participants who fit this description of them. You should note that some psychologists are uncomfortable with the term 'sex' and prefer you to use the word 'gender'. There is still some debate surrounding this. Sex is a biological term, and refers to the possession of certain chromosomes. Gender refers to behav-iour, so that if a person behaves in a 'masculine' fashion then we can call them masculine. Since we can't determine someone's sex by looking at them, we only have the way they act and dress as a guide. This is why many

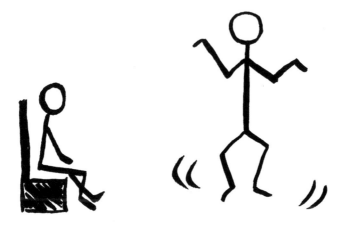

IF YOUR PARTICIPANT IS NOT
VERY TALKATIVE, DO NOT TRY
DANCING TO LIVEN THEM UP...

psychologists prefer the term 'gender'. However, in most cases, gender and sex coincide, which is why there is some argument.

Be aware that you might also refer to your participants as respondents if they have completed questionnaires for you. They have responded, so they are respondents. If you have interviewed them, you can call them interviewees. The word 'subject' has fallen out of usage of late, for various political reasons, although it is still strictly correct in the case of an experiment where a person has been *subjected to* some kind of manipulation, such as being put into a particular group or condition.

Materials or apparatus

This is where you describe any special materials or equipment that you used. If you used materials (stimuli, questionnaires, and so on) but no apparatus, label the section 'Materials'. If you used apparatus but no materials (much less likely), the section should be called 'Apparatus'.

When both are used, the section can be entitled 'Apparatus and Materials'. Note also that some people prefer a separate section known as 'Measures' where you have used questionnaires for some kind of survey.

Whatever this section ends up being called, it is only a description of what you used, and how they were created. It is *not* where you describe what you did with the materials or apparatus. Therefore, you would explain that you had a list of 20 nouns of a particular frequency of occurrence. You would *not* explain here how long your participants were exposed to the words, which is *procedural* detail.

You do not need to mention that you used pens, or blank paper, or a clipboard, or a table and chair. Of course, if you have used a very special sort of pen which is essential for the study, then you need to describe it, but this is exceedingly rare. Generally, you can avoid giving details of things which are not crucial to describe. It is true that you might have used paper and a pen, but would the results be different if someone used a pencil instead? Almost certainly not, which is why you do not need to mention it. Remember that the purpose of a Methods section is to ensure that someone else could try to replicate your study. Therefore, you only need to tell them about things which they should try to copy if they attempt to obtain the same findings by running your study again.

You must describe, in detail, any stimuli you use, or any questionnaires, or any hardware or software which is not commercially available *and* well known. There is no need to give a complete list of all stimuli (e.g. every word in a list of 250 of them), since you can list them in full in an appendix, but you should describe the *characteristics* of your stimuli, with examples. Don't just say, 'A questionnaire was used (see Appendix).' This tells the reader nothing about the nature of the questionnaire. Table 3 outlines what you should report for each common type of stimulus or apparatus, but is not an exhaustive list.

Procedure

This is where you explain what you did with your materials. You have already described the materials in the previous section. Don't introduce any new materials here. Simply tell a story of what happened to the participants, in chronological order. You don't need to explain things like the nature/layout of the room, unless they are essential to an understanding of the research. This is essentially where you explain what you and your participants *did*. You almost certainly will have some standardised instructions which you will have given to your participants, or read to them. Most

Table 3   Describing Stimuli and Apparatus

Stimuli or Apparatus	*Main Features to Describe*
word list	number, type (concrete noun, etc), where selected from, typeface/font/size in which presented
physical apparatus, such as a tapping-board or a mirror-drawing kit	full physical description, including dimensions and usually a diagram
physical apparatus such as a video camera	details, such as make and model
questionnaire	number of questions, types of questions, details of any subscales contained within, examples of questions of each type, details of any measurement scales, such as 'five-point Likert-type'
pictures or photographs	size presented, what the pictures are of, number, whether line diagrams or not, with examples
sounds	number, amplitude, frequency, and other physical or perceptual properties
music	name the pieces, the composers/bands, and, in the case of classical music, the orchestra and conductor; explain what the music is generally like for the readers who are not familiar with it, for example 'hip-hop' or 'guitar-based rock'
smells	you should give details of concentration (e.g. parts per million) and name the company/brand and descriptor for the odour

instructions can be turned into Procedure sections quite easily. If your instructions are clear and unambiguous, then there is no reason to have a Procedure section which is anything but.

Let's take an example. This is an excerpt from some instructions:

> You will be given three questionnaires to complete, each containing ten questions. In the first questionnaire, please answer each question by circling the statement which best applies to you. You should select only one statement. In the second questionnaire, you are asked to rank some leisure

pursuits in order of interest to you. Therefore, please write '1' next to the most interesting to you, followed by '2' and so on, until you have ranked them all. In the third questionnaire, you are asked questions about your health. Below each question is space for you to write whatever you like in response to the question. There are no right and wrong answers to any of the questions you are being presented with; we are interested in your opinions and beliefs.

Now, this can be converted into a Procedure section by simply altering the grammar so that the reader is not being addressed directly:

> Respondents were informed that they were to be given three questionnaires, each containing ten questions. They were told that in the first questionnaire they were to answer each question by circling the statement which best applied to them, selecting one statement only. In the second questionnaire, they were to rank some leisure pursuits in order of interest to them. Therefore, they were to write '1' next to the most interesting to them, followed by '2' and so on, until all were ranked. In the third questionnaire, participants were asked questions about their health. They were told that below each question was space for them to write whatever they wished in response to the question. They were specifically informed that there were no right and wrong answers to any of the questions and that the researchers were interested in their opinions and beliefs.

All you would now have to do is add some information about debriefing participants and whatever else is necessary, depending upon what you actually did. Hopefully you can now see how easy it is to write a procedure section. Of course, if you don't have any instructions, then it isn't. Having said that, it is hard to conceive of research where the participants do not receive any instructions. The exception is observational research.

In observational research, you sometimes do not have participants as such. The people you are observing are often not really taking part. They are simply doing what they would normally be doing. You are watching and recording their behaviour. In cases like this, you generally do not have any instructions. However, this does not mean that there is no procedure. You still *did* something that needs to be described. The nature of the observation process should be outlined. This includes the details of the time and place of the observation (unless in a laboratory), and what you recorded and how. If you are recording the difference between males and females in road-crossing behaviour, you must explain exactly how you defined the behaviours you are looking at and how you recorded them.

Replicability

Replicability is the key issue to writing a Method section. A write-up is successful if someone else can read what you have written and go away and do the same thing that you did. If they can't, you have got something wrong. All of the detail must be there to allow the reader to try to carry out research in the same way as you, so that they can check your findings. It's okay to have the specific detail in an appendix, but putting your questionnaire into an appendix is not an excuse for having an empty Materials section. You must still describe the general characteristics of the questionnaire in your Materials section. The reader might not be able to do exactly the same research as you from reading your Method, but they should be able to do something *very similar* in respect of the important detail.

The best way to check on this is to get someone else to read your Method. Preferably, they should not be another psychology student, and certainly not someone who might have been involved in the work you did, either as a researcher or participant. If you can, ask someone who knows nothing about psychology (but be aware that you might have to explain the Design to them). Ask them if they understood what they read. If they did not, think about how you can clarify some of the points you have made, in writing. If they say that they have understood it, don't leave it there. Test that out. Take away the written Method, and ask them to tell you, in logical order, what you did to whom, with what, and when and how. If they can't, then they didn't follow what you wrote. Don't blame them; go back to what you have written and change it to make it simpler and clearer.

The best time to write a Method section is whilst you are actively engaged in the research. It is easy to forget some small details (which could turn out to be important) if you find yourself writing about what you did weeks or months after you did it. Don't put off until tomorrow what you can do today, because you could find that, in the throes of doing research, you actually have a very poor memory of what happened yesterday!

Results

This is where you give the details of the statistical analysis you have conducted. There are very specific ways in which you should report the results of statistical tests, and it is so easy to get this wrong. What follows is not the *only* way to write a results section, but it is one way, and a perfectly acceptable way in the eyes of most psychologists.

The first golden rule is that you must not think of a results section as a place for numbers without words. Rather, it is a place for words where numbers also appear. First and foremost, you should be explaining your results in words. The numbers are there only to support and illustrate and to provide evidence for what you are saying. Therefore a table and a graph with no verbal explanation equates to a failed Results section.

The order in which you should present material in a Results section is generally this: introductory statement; descriptive statistics; introductory statement for inferential statistics; inferential statistics; graphical illustration, where appropriate; summary of results. Note that these are *not* sub-headings within the section. These are simply a description of what goes where.

So, you begin by introducing the data. It is often the case that you will have to remove some data because they are aberrant. Outliers might have to be trimmed. Mention this, so that it is clear why you now have fewer participants than you reported earlier. Similarly, you might have transformed the data to make them approximate a normal distribution. This should also be explained.

It is then usually necessary to give descriptive statistics (most commonly means and standard deviations) for your data. Do not give a list of raw data, under any circumstances. If you have a complex design, it is best to make sure that you are presenting descriptives for any sub-groups that you have. For example, if you have an ANOVA design with sex as one IV (two levels, of course) and condition as another (let's choose two levels again), then you should be showing the mean performance of males in each condition separately and the mean performance of females in each condition also. So, given that there are four cells in the design, there should be four sets of descriptives. It's OK to present the descriptives for the main effects as well; just don't leave out those for the cells of the design. Therefore, in this example, there would be six sets of means and SDs to present in total. It is best to present them in a table like this (although you would usually give statistics to two decimal places):

	Male (SD)	Female (SD)	Collapsed Mean (SD)
Condition One	34 (1)	32 (1)	33 (1)
Condition Two	38 (3)	42 (3)	40 (3)
Collapsed Mean (SD)	36 (2)	37 (2)	

You might not be familiar with the concept of collapsing. This simply means that you look at one dimension of the data without regard to the others. So, the collapsed mean for males, in this example, pays no regard to the condition. Similarly, the collapsed mean for Condition One pays no regard to the sex of the participants. It's like an average average, if you like. When you describe main effects in an ANOVA, you are always collapsing over the other variables, by definition. You can even report main effects in this way. (Note that in this example I have left off the units of measurement. You must never do this. Always give the units, otherwise the data make no sense – you can do this in the title of the table.)

The next thing that you should do is introduce the inferential statistics. Mention the analysis performed and the variables it has been performed on. Then give the results of that analysis in words, with any numerical/statistical details in brackets. Exactly what you say depends upon the nature of the analysis. Table 4 gives some examples of the more common types.

Table 4 How to Report Some Common Inferential Statistics

Analysis	Reportage
chi-squared	A chi-squared test revealed a significant asymmetry across cells [χ^2 (4,N=112)=14.2; $p<0.01$].
t-tests	An independent t-test revealed that there was no difference between males and females in their recall scores [t=1.2, $df = 48$; $p>0.05$].
correlation	A Pearson's r test showed a statistically significant correlation between recall score and anagram solving ability ($r = .84$, N=30; $p<0.01$).
one-way ANOVA	A one-way ANOVA on reaction times across groups revealed a significant difference between one or more stimulus groups [$F(3,108)=5.46$; $p<0.01$].
two-way ANOVA	An analysis of variance revealed a significant main effect of age [$F(1,138)=10.21$; $p<0.001$] and of sex [$F(1,138)=5.22$; $p<0.05$]. There was also a statistically significant interaction between age and sex [$F(1,138)=7.48$; $p<0.01$].
regression	Multiple regression analysis was employed to ascertain the prediction of well-being from age, health status and body mass index, and a significant model was observed [$F(3,478)=18.22$; $p<0.001$] with an adjusted R-squared of 0.56. Age, health status and BMI beta values were 0.23 ($p<0.05$), 0.30 ($p<0.01$) and 0.48 ($p<0.001$) respectively, showing that BMI contributes the greatest prediction of the variance in the criterion and age the least.

There are a few things to note in Table 4. First, note the uses of brackets/ parentheses. Don't end up with round brackets inside other round brackets. It is messy and difficult to follow. If you only need one set, use round ones. If you need two sets, use round ones inside square ones. If you need three sets, you're probably doing something wrong! Secondly, don't forget to include degrees of freedom when reporting parametric tests. You should know what these are, but if not make sure that you learn. If you know what they are, it makes it easier for you to pluck them out of your ANOVA output tables and put them into the appropriate place in your statement of results. Most statistics books explain this concept. Your tutor will explain to you where to find the right numbers in a statistical output such as that given by SPSS. Also, do not mix up the 'greater than' or 'less than' symbols when you are reporting probability values. Here are some rules to help you.

- A statistically significant result should be associated with '$p < 0.05$'. This means that p is less than 0.05. You can remember this because the smaller, closed end of the symbol is pointing to the 'p'.
- The p value for a non-significant difference is usually reported '$p > 0.05$'. This means that p is greater than 0.05. You can remember this because the larger, open end of the symbol is pointing to the 'p'.
- Sometimes you can give exact 'p' values, rounded to two decimal places. In fact this is becoming standard practice since these days computer packages calculate exact values for us. Most of the time, you don't need to bother doing this with non-significant differences. You might do this with significant differences only. However, generally, it can be simpler to use the standard categories of 'p': 0.05, 0.01, 0.001, 0.0001.
- Sometimes you don't have any significant effects at all. In such cases, it is common for authors to summarise the details of this in one global statement. This is especially useful when you are reporting main effects and interactions derived from an analysis of variance. For example, you can lump all the non-significant effects together by explaining that the F-ratios for all of these effects were very small. Since Fs less than 4.0 are usually non-significant, the reader will understand this if you present this. For example: 'There were no main effects of age, sex, or task complexity, nor any significant interactions between these variables ($Fs < 4$).'

You should also note that I have not included details of reporting the *post hoc* tests you might need to perform after an analysis of variance. Don't forget to run *post hoc* tests where appropriate, and report them. Most books on statistical analysis tell you about these, and Dancey & Reidy (2002) actually tell you how to write them up in your Results.

Graphs and diagrams

Try to resist the temptation to think that a report is not complete unless you have a graph or some sort of pictorial representation of the results. Look in most journal articles, and you will probably find that the majority do not. The rule to follow is that (unless you are told otherwise by your tutors) you only supply a diagram or graph where doing so actually helps the reader to understand the data you have, or your descriptive statistics. Most of the time, your analysis will have been quite simple, and so you must ask yourself whether it helps to paint a picture (almost literally!).

Generally, three or fewer means or other summary statistics do not need representing graphically. One common problem in reports is that students create pie charts for three or even two percentages. This is very unnecessary; in fact some readers might find it patronising. For example:

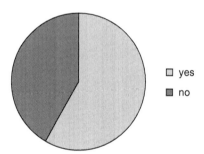

This pie chart is based on two percentages. These are 58 per cent and 42 per cent. Do you need help to imagine these numbers? I think I know the answer. Well, your reader does not need that help either. Even with three percentages (for example 60 per cent left-wing, 35 per cent right-wing, 5 per cent other), it's unlikely that you'll need help to conceptualise the relationship between the numbers. The same goes for block graphs of means. Generally, four or more and it's OK to give a graph, fewer than that and it's not. There are exceptions to this, as there are to most things, but this rule does normally apply.

Don't forget, however, that when you have an interaction between variables in an analysis of variance, you really ought to create a graph to show this. Again, this is a general rule only. Make sure that all of the appropriate lines and axes are properly labelled, and that there is a title for the graph which explains what it shows. Try to aim for a short title which mentions the variables involved.

You might like to include a scatterplot where you have found a significant relationship between two key variables, but you may also find that you advised by your tutor that this is not necessary. This is largely a matter of opinion, and you should follow the instructions given by your lecturers in this respect.

Generally, you should avoid using fancy shading options and garish colours when producing graphical representations of data. You will not normally gain additional marks for this, and in fact at times the reader can be put off by overly artistic graphs. Three-dimensional perspective is usually completely unnecessary. As long as you have a simple diagram or graph which is clear and easy to understand, try to resist doing anything else to it. Just because your word processor will do amazing things does not mean that you always have to take advantage of all of its functions.

Finally, *never* plot a graph of individual participants on the horizontal axis and their scores on the vertical. Basically, such a graph tells you nothing at all, because the scores are not ordered in any way. In addition, such graphs become massive when you have a large number of participants and would probably stretch across a few pages.

Ending your results

If you have reported a number of findings, it might be advisable to summarise your results in a short sentence or two at the end of the section. You should normally not end with numbers or pictorial representations of data, but with some words, just as you should never begin with anything other than words. Remember: results sections are primarily where you should be explaining your findings in words, with pictures and tables merely supporting the verbal.

Discussion

Start your discussion with a general statement which summarises your results, in words only. Do not give values of *t* or F or *p* values. Once you have done this, you can now go on to discuss the extent to which your findings are in keeping with your hypothesis/hypotheses, and in keeping with what other researchers have found. Think about the consequences of your results for existing theories. You might need to adapt current theories in the light of your findings, and generate a new theory or model of your own. The most important thing to remember is that your Discussion section is where you consider and infer things from your results. You take the findings, and ponder over what they might tell us. Never do this in the Results section itself, where you should only give the 'facts' without interpretation.

Once this is done, you might then need to comment on any issues which might cast doubt on your findings. Do not scrape the bottom of the barrel to find reasons why your results might be dubious. This is silly. Instead, mention only potential problems which might have influenced your data. What do we mean by this? This is best demonstrated by examples.

- Mention any potentially confounding variables. For instance, you might have noticed that your two conditions have people of different ages in them. One group might be older than the other. This might mean that your observed difference is only an age difference, not due to your independent variable. Or you might have compared two age groups on a vocabulary task, only to find that one age group came from a school year which has just been taking part in a spelling competition whereas the other group did not. Again, something could be 'interfering' with your hoped-for result.
- Another problem might be that you discovered, after the research was conducted, that some participants may have misunderstood the instructions.
- Yet another example might be where participants could have ignored your instructions and done 'their own thing' without you being aware. You can't control what happens in people's minds, and so although you instruct people to form mental images of words and nothing else they might additionally be constructing rhyming associations between the words. This is something probably worth mentioning.

Most of all, don't clutch at straws. If there's nothing obviously wrong with your research, that's actually something to be celebrated. Only bring up problems where there might be some.

Don't rely on the age-old criticisms of research such as 'the results may have been different had the sample size been larger'. This is the most common problem with research reported by students, and you almost never get any credit for this, in fact you are quite likely to lose marks for it. There are a number of reasons. First, if you have reported a statistically significant difference or relationship, then the sample size has been taken into account already in the formula. Secondly, you should not be writing-up research with a sample size which is too small. A good researcher carries on collecting data until the sample size is large enough. (Earlier in this book, in Chapter 1, I mentioned power analysis.) Thirdly, no sample size is ever good enough, in theory. You can argue that the results would be different with a larger sample size even if you had a million participants! What about all the other people on earth? Even if you tested everyone on earth, it is still possible to argue that this is not enough because you haven't tested all the people who are now dead, and all of the people still to be born. Where do you stop?

Another common mistake that students make is to mention a flaw which is likely to have applied to all participants, no matter which condition or group they were in. The main reason for pointing out flaws or confounding variables is that they might have affected the observed result, either causing no difference to appear when there really is one, or making one appear that is not 'real'. However, if a flaw probably affected *everyone equally*, then it is of less relevance. Therefore, mild background noise of a constant level in a testing room, which was the same throughout the testing situation, is often not going to be *that* important. Of course, if your experiment involves playing sounds to people at different volumes, then suddenly it becomes relevant because the low-volume groups would have probably also heard the background noise whereas the high-volume groups would not. Thus, some participants might have been distracted more than others, and this distraction is likely to be systematic, rather than random. This is the key. A systematic flaw, rather than a random one, which has probably affected one group more than another, is almost certainly worth reporting. Otherwise, it might not be.

Next, you would normally suggest further research which might be conducted into the area under discussion. It is important, as always, to remain faithful to the topic, and not to let your imagination run away with you. Make sure that any further research you suggest is going to find out something more about the *specific* topic at hand, not just the general area of research. Think about ways of adapting your study to correct any problems you have found, or ways of changing questions or stimuli which would further back up your findings. No matter what you do, don't leave the country! You might wonder what I mean by this. Well, it's common for students to think that introducing a cross-cultural element is a good way to suggest further research. I have lost count of the number of reports I have read containing a statement like 'It would be interesting to see if the same findings apply in other countries or in other ethnic groups.' Well, it might be interesting, but would it be relevant, or would you simply be suggesting a completely new strand of research, outside the current remit? Unless you have a strong reason (and usually *evidence*) to believe that the things you are researching might actually differ across cultures, don't bring it up. Similarly, don't suggest that the research should be carried out on different age groups, unless you can argue that it is important and would not pull the research away from the topic into developmental psychology! The same applies to student participants. It is true that research carried out on students *might* be limited in how much it can be generalised, but it isn't necessarily *always* so. If you have conducted research on attitudes to late-night parties, then students would probably give different answers from a group of over-80s or a group of independent parents. However, if you have conducted research on pattern-recognition, or the effects of lavender essential oil on problem-solving activity, then there is probably no good reason to think that students differ from anyone else (except, of course, in the fact that as people age their sense of smell and their vision usually deteriorate, and students tend to be relatively young, on average).

Obviously, the best way to get a sense of how to correctly identify future research which is on-topic is to read original journal articles. Generally, however, you will be thinking along the right lines if you entertain ideas in the same vein as these questions:

- Can you change the stimuli and still get the same effects, e.g. swapping pictures for words or sounds?
- Can you introduce a control group of some sort which you didn't have before?
- Can you try extending the parameters of the study, perhaps by having more groups?
- Can you pick up on themes brought up by your participants in the interviews?

Try to end your Discussion by summarising the research in a few words, and making some statement about the need for research in this area. Don't try to demonstrate that need by simply saying it, nor by saying that the area of research is 'interesting'. Whether or not something is interesting is a matter of opinion. You must relate, wherever possible, the area of research to some real-life problem or mystery which needs to be solved. If the findings of research like yours can be applied to some greater concern in the world, here's where you say so. Essentially, you are leaving the reader with your most important point. Politicians and speech-makers call this the 'take-home message'.

Sometimes the take-home message is best phrased in terms of the practical applications of the research which has been conducted. That is, you leave the reader with a good sense of why your research has been worthwhile. Some research seems very abstract, and cannot be easily demonstrated to be applicable to practical problems in real life. However, most research findings can be applied to some question that needs answering. Of course, some research should only be conducted if it is clearly applied in focus, especially research involving medical patients. In fact, you are unlikely to achieve ethical clearance from an external committee unless you can demonstrate this. Research generates knowledge and information. Ask yourself who might benefit from the information you have created at the end of your study. Will your findings help doctors understand deaf patients better, or social workers appreciate the differences between Bosnian men and women, or learner drivers judge distances better? If so, say so.

Generalising Your Findings

It is not uncommon for researchers to suggest how their findings might be generalised to other groups of participants or to other contexts or scenarios. There is a fine balance between sensible generalisations and ridiculous claims, so be careful how you address this issue if you tackle it in your Discussion section. In qualitative research, much of the problem is taken away from you, since one of the principles of qualitative paradigms is that generalising findings is not usually desirable. The aim of qualitative research is often only to describe and explain participants' thoughts and feelings on a particular issue, not to describe and explain those of other people or to suggest how people might think about another, separate issue.

In the case of experimental or quantitative research, there is often an in-built hope that the research findings can apply in similar situations with other groups of people. This whole aspect of the research is tied in with the notion of representativeness of the sample of participants. If you have sampled what you believed to be a representative cross-section of the public, then you are on relatively safe ground if you assume that your results will apply to the people that you haven't sampled. However, this interacts with the nature of what you are studying. With most cognitive or physiological experiments, you can probably assume that everyone is roughly the same. To most psychologists, memory is memory, audition is audition, and heart-rate is heart-rate, no matter who takes part in the research, because human beings have roughly the same body parts and brain areas of roughly the same size which function in roughly the same way in all people (otherwise surgeons would never be able to learn about the body from one set of people and apply it to their future patients!). There are exceptions to this, such as the fact that men and women often differ in the relative sizes of the left and right hemispheres of the brain, but the rule does generally hold.

However, you should always reflect on what *representative* actually means. It does not usually imply that a sample represents all people, but rather all people of a particular type. Thus you can have a representative sample of Welsh miners, or physically disabled people, or opera singers, but getting a representative sample of people in general is probably impossible. Therefore, be careful that you don't try to assume that a set of attitudes observed in white people will be the same in black people, or that you can map the observed behaviour of teenagers on to that of 'thirty-somethings'.

References

For many students, referencing is one of the most difficult things to get right. Most departments will expect you to use APA formats for referencing and citing. Therefore, what follows is current APA style. It changes slightly from time to time, but never dramatically. If your department prefers you to use some other form of referencing such as Harvard, then please follow their guidelines instead. However, many journals and most departments prefer the use of APA style.

Before we start with the detail, it is important to note the difference between a citation and a reference. A *citation* is the mention of some authors, along with a date, in the main text of an article or report. A *reference* is the full listing of that research, found at the back of an essay or report. It is there so that someone can go to their library and read the same article that you have. It allows them to check that you have fairly and accurately reported someone else's research, theories or conclusions.

Citation

Citing is relatively easy. The simplest form is where there is one author. Therefore, this book would be cited as Forshaw (2004). Note that there are two ways of doing this, depending upon the sentence around it:

According to Forshaw (2004), many key journals use APA referencing style.

Many key journals use APA referencing style (Forshaw, 2004).

Multiple authors are dealt with as you might expect. If an article has two authors, name them thus: Smith & Smith (1999). When a paper has several authors, give all of them the first time you mention the paper and then use *et al.* after that. Make sure you include the full stop after the 'al' because it is short for *alia*, Latin for 'others'. Herein lies another important point. Don't mistakenly use *et al.* when there are only two authors in total. 'Others' means 'more than one other'!

If you want to cite a collection of articles on a subject as evidence, you should do so in brackets with semi-colons between citations. Put them in alphabetical order. Here is an example. 'Many authors have argued that people living in smaller houses are more likely to enjoy cheese (Arnold & Fisk, 1967; Finch, 1990; Reading & Holmes, 2001).'

If you are citing two or more papers by the same author(s) in the same year, you use letters after the date to distinguish them. Therefore, if Postman has published three papers in the same year, you might have three citations: first Postman (2000a), then at some other point you might mention Postman (2000b), and lastly Postman (2000c). In your References you would make a similar distinction. Don't do this unless all of the authors are exactly the same. Therefore, Postman & Letterman (1999) and Letterman & Postman (1999) are entirely separate and different and there is no confusion, therefore no need to add any letters. Occasionally, I have seen reports where a student has lifted a reference from a book or an article and has naïvely copied the letter too, even when they are only citing one paper in that year by that particular author. This is a dead giveaway that the student has not actually read the original and has cheated by taking the detail from a book without citing the source.

One issue which is worth mentioning also is that of *secondary citation*. When you read a summary of research from a book rather than the original paper, you should indicate this, as the case above partly demonstrates. If you read about Chipolata & Farinheira (1987) in a book by Chorizo (1992), you should show this as follows:

'Most studies of sausage-eating behaviour have indicated that people prefer spiced to unspiced meat products (Chipolata & Farinheira, 1987, cited in Chorizo, 1992).'

Then you give *only* a reference for Chorizo in your References section. Simple as that!

Referencing

There are numerous rules about different kinds of references, but there are two main types of reference you will encounter which you absolutely must learn about. These are books and journal articles. For more detail, read more about referencing in the *Publication Manual of the American Psychological Association* (2001), which your library is likely to have a copy of.

For books, the reference looks like this:

Grump, N. E. (2000). *Twigs, Sprigs and Pigs: A Guide to Rearing Forest Swine.* London: Farm Press.

Don't forget to include the place of publication and the publisher, and don't forget to italicise the title of the book.

For journal articles, this is the standard format:

Turn, A. & Turnabout, C. (2002). Country Dancing Performance as a Function of Age and Height, *Journal of Contemporary Fun, 12,* 202–206.

Note here that the journal title and volume number are italicised, *not* the title of the article. Don't forget to include the page numbers.

More things to remember about references

- A References section is not the same thing as a Bibliography. *Reports have References, not Bibliographies.* A References list gives details of sources you have *cited.* A Bibliography is a list of things the reader might like to consult because they are relevant to the topic. It's like a Further Reading list, which you'll find at the back of this book, *after* the References.
- A References section should only contain full references for the literature that you have cited: nothing else. Similarly, everything that you have cited should be listed in your References section. There should be a perfect match between the two.
- Don't include books or articles that you have read but not cited.
- Double-check to make sure that your References list is in alphabetical order. If you have two Smiths with the same initials (e.g. Smith, 1988 and Smith, 2000), refer to them in date order. If the initials are different because they are different people called Smith, put them in alphabetical order of the initials.
- Don't cite research by saying things like 'a researcher at the University of California ... 'or 'a psychologist called Smith conducted a study ... ', and so on. This is unnecessary information. Also, don't cite first names in the main body of text, unless you need to distinguish between authors with the same surname. Therefore, you could get away with 'M. Eysenck' and 'H. Eysenck' mentioned thus if you are citing both

authors. Note, however, that I have given the initials in order to distinguish, *not* the full first names.

- Don't change people's names. Muller is not the same as Müller. Learn to use the functions of your word-processing package which allow you to insert an umlaut where necessary, or a grave accent, or whatever is needed. In modern versions of *Microsoft Word*, go to the menu bar, select Insert, then Symbol. A list of characters will appear. Find the one you want, click on Insert, then Close. It is easy to get this right, and it shows respect for others and a keen eye for detail.

Appendices

Appendices should be clearly labelled and clearly referred to in the text. It's not rare for people to mix up their appendices, referring the reader to Appendix A when the relevant material is actually to be found in Appendix B! Similarly, students often stick everything but the kitchen sink into a solitary appendix which is then pages and pages long and almost impossible to find things in. If you have a lot of material which needs to be presented in appendices, you should make separate appendices for each item or set of items. In the main body of your report, the first appendix referred to should be Appendix One. Keep to numerical order if you have many appendices (or if you prefer you can have Appendix A, B, C, and so on.) Generally, you don't need to put raw data in an appendix unless you are asked to do so. You might be asked to put details of statistical analysis in an appendix, and you should always include copies of materials, unless they are particularly long, in which case you should ask your supervisor for their opinion.

If you have included any letters to participants or other correspondence, make sure that people and organisations are not identifiable by name. It is not only a courtesy to anonymise your participants. You may well be contravening law if you do not.

⊞ QUALITATIVE REPORTS

Qualitative research is, in many senses, quite different from that which is quantitative in nature, and so this is reflected in the writing-up process. Although there is some overlap between the standard methods of writing up quantitative and qualitative reports, there are also significant discrepancies. In psychology, qualitative research is quite a new way of doing things, and so new ways of writing-up are also required. In this section, you will find information on how to write up qualitative work. Do bear in mind, however, that the rules are not strict ones. There are many acceptable ways to write up qualitative research. Therefore, what follows is quite general, and you are strongly advised to talk about the write-up carefully with your supervisor.

The First Person

It is usually quite acceptable to use the first person ('I') when writing up qualitative research, very much contrary to when reporting experimental or quantitative work.

Introduction

The Introduction is not greatly different from that you would produce for quantitative methods, but towards the end of the section you should include, in your rationale, some explanation of the particular method you have used and why it is particularly appropriate for what you have been researching. After all, your ethos and your method and the topic under investigation are all tied up together. Remember that you don't really have hypotheses as such either. Generally, if you are conducting the kind of qualitative research where you are trying out ideas or hunches, you might want to include a statement of a 'research question'. Don't refer to it as an hypothesis.

Methods

Replicability is not really an aim of qualitative research at all, but this does not mean that you should fail to explain your methods in enough detail that someone could follow up for research. Similarly, a good qualitative report still contains information about the what, how, where and when of things. By clearly setting out what you did you make it easier for the reader to actually understand what your research is all about. So, in this sense, you would be well advised to try to aim for a description of your methods which still has some of the rigour and clarity of a quantitative write-up.

In qualitative work, the 'who', 'when' and 'where' is often seen as just as important as the 'what'. What I mean by this is that qualitative researchers accept that the context of an investigation and the personal characteristics of the investigators and 'participants' can strongly dictate the nature of the findings. Therefore you should explain what your relationship to your interviewees might be (friends, family, complete strangers and so on), and when and in what contexts you conducted your research. If you are asking people about their thoughts about cod fishing, you should mention if there has just been a European-wide embargo on it recently put into place and reported in the popular press. To leave this detail out would be to give a false impression of the context of your research.

Some words should normally be used up on what is often called 'reflex-ivity'. This is the idea that you aim to be as honest as possible to the reader as to your own personal thoughts on the issue under investigation and what your interest in the research actually is. Not every qualitative re-searcher insists on such a section, and psychologists argue as to whether a separate subsection is required or simply some discussion of the issue in the text, but most do seem to think that you should deal with this, even if only briefly.

Results/Analysis/Discussion

It is not uncommon to fuse the Results and Discussion sections together, because it is unwieldy to report qualitative findings (in the form of quota-tions from transcripts) separately from the suggested 'meaning' or the researcher's interpretations of them.

Give examples of the themes you extract from data using two or three short quotations for each, and providing line and paragraph numbers so that the reader can look at these in your actual transcripts. Don't give dozens of examples of each point. Make your examples as short as is physically possible, and select them carefully.

Be careful not to go beyond your data when trying to make conclusions about the research. The purpose of most qualitative research is not to generate 'grand theory' about human behaviour. Mostly, it is about offering interpretations of *what happened, when it happened, in the people that it happened to*. Don't make generalisations, and don't assume that you'll be bound to find the same thing again if you repeat the research. This has implications for how you deal with the closing part of the Discussion, in that you will have to curb the tendency to use your findings to explain what people in general might think. For the most part, stick to dealing with the findings within the specific circumstances under which you conducted the study.

You might also revisit the issue of reflexivity here, offering the reader any new thoughts you have about the research after having conducted it, and how you have changed as a result of being involved in the process. Research changes things, whether you like it or not, and you and your participants will probably alter in some ways as a consequence of living through the experience of the research process.

⌗ FIRST, SECOND AND THIRD DRAFTS

Some people seem able to simply write things off the cuff which display all the hallmarks of brilliance. It is possible that you are one of those. However, it is much more likely that you will need to revisit and change what you have written over time, amending, rewriting, deleting, adding, and moving text to create the final version.

I always advise students to begin by writing *anything*. It doesn't have to be good, but it has to be *something*. There's a reason for this; you can't change nothing. You can't edit nothing. Once you have something, you can begin working on it. This *something* is your first draft.

Revisions of a piece of work can take many forms. Some people like to make passes through the text looking for different things each time. That way you are more likely to spot any problems because you are only looking for one thing at once. So, you might run through the text checking that it flows from sentence to sentence, then from paragraph to paragraph. In another pass you can check for repetition. It is often the case that when you read through something that you have written you find that you have used the same word over and over again. We all have our 'favourite' words which keep cropping up in our speech and writing, and which change over time like clothing fashions. However, a text which repeatedly uses the same word becomes quite boring to the reader and even confusing. The sign of a good writer is someone who can find many words to say the same thing.

Don't be afraid to change what you have written. Just keep a copy so that if you change your mind and feel that you have fixed something which wasn't broken you can revert to the earlier version.

Between revisions, leave a few days or even weeks. When you come back to a piece that you have written, after enough time for you to partly forget about it, you see all sorts of things which you have never seen before. Occasionally you see the error of your ways, but sometimes you get a sense of having produced a written piece which is actually quite good and of which you are proud.

With practice, you will learn when to stop rewriting. Endless drafts are not helpful. You will never create a piece that is perfect, so you must be willing to accept that there comes a point when tweaking your work no longer makes it better. Everyone who creates must learn this skill, whether they are a novelist, scientist, painter or musician. There's a good reason why the English language has a large number of phrases to describe messing with things which are already fine, such as 'over-egging the pudding' and 'gilding the lily'.

⊞ COMMON MISTAKES

There are thousands of mistakes which students make and which turn up again and again in research reports. It is not possible to list all of them, but here is a list of some of the most frequent ones, and those which usually can make a difference to the mark given to a piece of work. Some are mistakes of English, others errors of knowledge, but all are important in their own way. Note that if you use spelling and grammar checkers in your word-processing package you are not guaranteed to avoid mistakes. Sometimes a spellchecker will help you to make errors! Computers are quite stupid, and they cannot work out what you mean to say. A good, old-fashioned dictionary is a great tool, and you would be well advised to use one. If you accidentally type 'so' instead of 'to', the spellchecker will not notice it. Equally, do not merrily click on everything the spellchecker suggests. Sometimes it doesn't know a word, even though it's a real one. It might want to change that word. This is why a dictionary is important.

Affect and Effect

Many people regularly confuse these words. It doesn't help that both of them can be nouns and both can be verbs. Usually, however, affect is used as a verb and effect as a noun. Therefore, the most common uses of the words are as in these examples:

- Alcohol affects how people behave.
- Alcohol has an effect on how people behave.

Data

'Data' is plural. 'Datum' is singular. Therefore, a single number is a datum. A set of numbers is data. People often get around this by saying 'data point', but this is not really correct, since a data point is a datum.

Experiment and Study

Only describe your work as an experiment if it actually is one! If you have manipulated a variable or variables, and controlled other aspects of the research, then you have an experiment on your hands. If not, you do not. If you can't correctly describe your research using the word 'experiment', then use another word instead, like 'study'.

Qualitative, correlational or regressional work cannot be experimental, and so should never be described as such. Some observational work might be experimental, but only where you are interfering with the environment and people that you are observing. If you are conducting a natural observation, where you simply label what is happening anyway, without any intervention from you, then this cannot be experimental.

Joining Words Together

It is increasingly common for some students to join words together, for some mysterious reason. 'A lot' is two words. 'As well' is two words. However, do note the following:

- When you mean 'perhaps', 'maybe' is one word.
- When you are saying that your best friend may be a fish, 'may be' is two words.

Incorrect Apostrophes

I would estimate that around half of university students (and a few lecturers!) make mistakes surrounding the use of apostrophes. Here are some simple rules.

Plurals do not take apostrophes. 'One variable, two variables.' 'One study, two studies.' Next time you go shopping, see how many of these you can spot on your travels, all of which are incorrect: pizza's, tomato's, kebab's, cauliflower's, shirt's, and so on. Also, don't refer to decades using an apostrophe; the correct form is 1970s, 1980s, 1990s, and so on.

It's/its confuses many people. Basically, 'it's' should never appear in an essay or report. It is short for 'it is'. In that case, write 'it is'. When you indicate a possessive (something owning something), use 'its'. Therefore, 'the dog was chewing its bone.'

Most of the time, apostrophes indicate possession. Where the apostrophe goes depends on who is doing the possessing. Or, rather, how many people are doing the possessing. Therefore:

- I can point to the dog's kennel.
- I can point to the dogs' kennel.

In the first case, there is one dog, in the second case there is an unspecified number of dogs, but definitely more than one.

If you are thinking this is all very pedantic and unnecessary, I sympathise, but I would point out to you that sometimes the apostrophe makes all the difference. Compare these two statements:

- I had no food, so I ate the dog's.
- I had no food, so I ate the dogs.

The first situation is nasty and strange, but legal. The second is a criminal offence in Britain.

Incorrect Sentences

Writing incomplete sentences can occur because of errors in using commas, but also owing to a mistake in the use of the word 'being'.

Commas cannot be used to join together two clauses which are complete sentences in themselves. They are normally only used to separate different parts (clauses) of a single sentence. This is best explained by means of examples.

- I am an idiot. I lost my keys. This is *correct*, because both are complete sentences.
- I am an idiot; I lost my keys. This is *correct*, because you can use a semi-colon to join complete sentences which relate closely to each other.
- I am an idiot, I lost my keys. This is *incorrect*. You cannot use a comma here.

- Sadly, I am an idiot. This is *correct*, because the bit before the comma is not a sentence.
- If you start a sentence with a word like 'however', 'unexpectedly', or 'therefore', you should immediately follow it with a comma.

It is very common for people to think that a sentence can hinge around the word 'being'. A lot of the time, sentences with this word in them are incorrect. For example, *you can't say*:

This being an example of his rudeness.

This is *wrong*, because it doesn't make sense when you read it on its own. Even when the sentence before it explains what you are talking about, you still can't write this, because each sentence has to make some sense without reading everything else around it.

Therefore this is also *wrong*:

He shouted loudly at me for no reason. This being an example of his rudeness.

In *all* cases like this, use a comma instead of the full stop between the sentences. Therefore:

He shouted loudly at me for no reason, this being an example of his rudeness.

This is *correct*.

Latin Phrases and Other Borrowings

The English language is full of borrowings from other languages. Sometimes this is for convenience, at other times because we can express something by using a foreign word better than in English. Using these correctly is important.

'e.g.' is used to indicate an example of something. It means *exempli gratia*, or 'an example for free'. Therefore you might say 'There are many people in my house, e.g. my friend Emma.' Emma is an *example* of a person in my house, but not the only one.

'i.e.' means *id est*, Latin for 'that is'. You use this as in 'There is one person in my house, i.e. my friend Emma.' Here, Emma is the *only* person in my house. She's *not* an example.

We use many other Latin phrases, of course, but these are the ones which are most often misused. Make sure that you *italicise* any Latin words or phrases that you use, and keep your use of 'e.g.' and 'i.e.' to an absolute minimum, especially 'e.g.', the deployment of which is considered to be a little lazy by some people.

We have borrowed quite a few words from German which are used in psychology, almost all of which are nouns. If you use these, you should be aware that in German all nouns take an initial capital. Therefore, we should write Gestalt, Zeitgeist, Weltanschauung, Schadenfreude, Zeitgeber, Einstellung, and so on.

Non-significant

The opposite of 'significant', in statistical terms, is 'non-significant'. It is also acceptable to say 'not significant'. *Never*, under any circumstances, say 'insignificant' or 'unsignificant'. 'Insignificant' means 'unimportant', which is not the same as 'non-significant'. You can have very important non-significant results. 'Unsignificant' is not even an English word, so you certainly should not be using that!

Number and Amount

This is a confusion which I find increasingly prevalent. The rule for using the words correctly is actually very simple. If you can count them, use 'number'. If you can't, use 'amount'. Therefore, you have a number of people, a number of fish and a number of stars. You have an amount of milk, an amount of jam, and an amount of dough. You have a number of milk bottles and jam jars, however, because you can count those. It doesn't matter if it would be extremely difficult to count something. If it is theoretically possible, use 'number'. Hence the example involving stars. You will hear the phrase 'an amount of people' quite a lot. It's a common mistake. You can count people. It would be very difficult to count the people in China, but it's possible. Therefore, China has a large *number* of people living in it. This relationship also applies when using the comparative terms 'less' and 'fewer'.

- There are fewer than eight people in this room. *Correct.*
- I wish I could eat less jam. *Correct.*

You can't have fewer jam, and you can't have less people, no matter what you might hear people saying!

Prefixes

Prefixes are not words in themselves, but are stuck on to the front of other words to modify them in some way. They must be stuck on the words, using a hyphen, and should never float on their own on the page. The most common mistakes are made with 'non' and 'extra'. These should appear with other words, as in 'non-significant' and 'extra-curricular'. If you are tempted to use 'extra' on its own, use 'additional' instead. Other common prefixes include 'co-', 'pre-', 'post-', 'ante-', and 'multi-'. Note also that 'non' is a Latin word, and *can* appear on its own in Latin phrases, as in *sine qua non* or *non sequitur.*

Presenting Numbers

When you write numbers, there is a rule of thumb as to whether you write the number in words or figures, e.g. 'five' or '5'.

- In Results sections, you will normally use the figures.
- In the other sections, numbers under 10 are usually written as words, and 10 or more are usually written in figures. So, you write 'eight', but you write '13'.
- When a sentence begins with a number, always write it in words. Sometimes it is better, however, to simply avoid writing a sentence in such a way that it begins with a number.
- Decimals should always be written in figures, as should page numbers or lists of numbers and sample sizes reported in your Participants sub-section.
- Use a hyphen to connect numbers up to 99 written as words (where appropriate). Therefore, you should write 'twenty-two' but 'six hundred and three'.

Proof

Never use the word 'proof'. Your results don't prove anything, no matter how good the research. It's a philosophical issue, but nevertheless you should be aware of it. Proof is absolute; if you prove something, that means it is true. You can't actually demonstrate that things are true. You can only show that things are untrue, by disproof or falsification. So, it's

OK to speak of disproving a hypothesis by showing results contrary to it, but you can't *prove* an hypothesis.

Beware of reports of research you encounter on TV or in newspapers. The word 'proof' is thrown about rather liberally, and we commonly hear of scientists 'proving' this or that. Quite simply, this is wrong. Apart from a few notable cases, journalists are not scientists, and are rarely aware of the nature of the philosophical debate on the nature of evidence and proof.

Reporting Probabilities

Never write 'p<0.000' or 'p=0.000'. This is not only completely wrong, but also shows that you simply don't understand probability. P can never be equal to zero, except in statistical theory. Some statistical software will give exactly these values in their outputs, but this is only because they cannot print more than three decimal places. There are more numbers beyond the 0s, but you can't see them. So, the computer throws up 'p=0.000', but the truth might be 'p=0.000912475832', or something similar. Therefore, whenever this happens, report instead 'p<0.001'. Those of you who understand the concept of rounding-up should be able to see why. If you don't, ask your tutor. But *never* just copy the p=0.000 into your report. It's wrong.

Separating Words

Just as some people seem to join words together, others seem compelled to tear them apart. All of the following are one word, not two or more: 'however', 'therefore', 'whereas', 'whereby', 'wherein', 'therein', 'thereby', 'inasmuch'. The last one is a very strange word to most people, but you will find it in your dictionary. Note that spellcheckers will not spot certain mistakes of this nature. If you accidentally separate the 'how' from the 'ever', your computer won't point this out to you because both of these parts are words in their own right. The same applies to every one of the words above.

Significant Differences

When reporting results, it is extremely common for students to state that their results were significant. This is incorrect. Results are just results. Findings are just findings. When you have conducted a statistical test of inference, you are looking to see if a difference or a relationship between groups or variables is significant. Therefore, this is what you should say. The following are both correct:

- A statistically significant difference was observed between older and younger participants' scores on the reaction time task.
- The relationship between age and vocabulary score was statistically significant.

Spelling IV and DV

Most people can spell 'variable', but they often make mistakes when spelling 'independent' and 'dependent'. Take note of these spellings. A psychologist uses these words a lot, and so it makes sense that he or she is able to spell them. Note that a spellchecker will allow 'dependant'. It is a word, but it is not the right word to describe a variable. It is a noun to describe a person who might rely on someone else for their finances or upkeep, such as someone's child or unemployed partner. See? Nothing to do with variables at all!

⌗ WHEN IT'S ALL OVER

You might wonder what there is left to say when your research is completed and the work handed in. Well, in the case of some student projects, the supervisor occasionally feels that the work is good enough to be edited and turned into an article for publication. They will tell you if this is the case. You should generally feel very proud if this happens, and should not decline such an offer in normal circumstances, since publishing a paper is something that very few students do, and as such it can greatly enhance your *curriculum vitae* and thus your employment and training prospects.

The normal process is for the supervisor to ask you for an electronic copy of your project write-up, and possibly your data, and to work on this to turn it into something more suitable for publication, editing, rewriting, re-analysing, and so on. Your help may be asked for at various points.

There are, it should be noted, a few issues that are important to be aware of. Reflecting on these should prevent problems later.

- You should always see a final copy of the paper to be submitted. If your name is on it, you should agree to what is being said. Whilst there will not normally be a problem, now and then a supervisor might either make an error of interpretation of the data, or even make claims which you feel are not quite something you personally agree with. Be polite but assertive should this very rare thing happen.

- It is generally accepted that your name will appear on any publication. Your supervisor ought to do this as a matter of course. Exactly whose name comes first is a matter of negotiation, but it is common practice for the supervisor to be placed first, usually because they have guided the work throughout and because the paper to be submitted will almost certainly have been worked on considerably by the lecturer concerned.
- Do not expect the paper to be published. It is best to be prepared for the worst. Only a small proportion of articles submitted are ever published. In the best situation there is about a one in five chance it will make it to print, but for some journals this is closer to just 5 per cent.
- Do not expect the paper to be published quickly. The usual process is for the paper to be submitted, and the editor of the journal reads it and decides if it is appropriate for that journal. The editor sends it to two or three reviewers who then read it, comment on it, and it goes back. If you are lucky, there is nothing to do after this. However, it is likely that the reviewers expect some more work to be done. You do the work, and it may have to go back to the reviewers again to check that they are now satisfied. If so, it will then enter the actual publication process. At best, the entire process will take around a year, at worst two or three.

REFERENCES

Bell, J. (1999). *Doing Your Research Project: A Guide for First-time Researchers in Education and Social Science,* third edition. Buckingham: Open University Press.

Dancey, C. P. & Reidy, J. (2003). *Statistics Without Maths for Psychology: Using SPSS for Windows,* second edition. Harlow: Pearson Prentice Hall.

Denscombe, M. (2002). *Ground Rules for Good Research: A 10-Point Guide for Social Researchers.* Buckingham: Open University Press.

Smith, J. A., Jarman, M. & Osborn, M. (1999). Doing Interpretative Phenomenological Analysis. In Murray, M. & Chamberlain, K. (eds.), *Qualitative Health Psychology: Theories & Methods.* London: Sage.

Sommer, R. & Sommer, B. (2002). *A Practical Guide to Behavioral Research: Tools and Techniques,* fifth edition. New York: Oxford University Press.

FURTHER READING

Ballenger, B. (2004). *The Curious Researcher: A Guide to Writing Research Papers*, fourth edition. New York: Pearson Longman.

Bell, J. (1999). *Doing Your Research Project: A Guide for First-time Researchers in Education and Social Science*, third edition. Buckingham: Open University Press.

Coolican, H. (2004) *Research Methods and Statistics in Psychology*, fourth edition. London: Hodder & Stoughton.

Dancey, C. P. & Reidy, J. (2002). *Statistics Without Maths for Psychology: Using SPSS for Windows*, second edition. Harlow: Pearson Prentice Hall.

Denscombe, M. (2002). *Ground Rules for Good Research: A 10 Point Guide for Social Researchers*. Buckingham: Open University Press.

Denscombe, M. (2003). *The Good Research Guide: For Small-scale Social Research Projects*, second edition. Buckingham: Open University Press.

Hayes, N. (2000). *Doing Psychological Research: Gathering and Analysing Data*. Buckingham: Open University Press.

Langdridge, D. (2004). *Introduction to Research Methods and Data Analysis in Psychology*. Harlow: Pearson/Prentice Hall.

Martin, D. W. (2000). *Doing Psychology Experiments*, fifth edition. Pacific Grove, CA: Brooks/Cole.

Pelham, B. W. (1999). *Conducting Experiments in Psychology: Measuring the Weight of Smoke*. Pacific Grove, CA: Brooks/Cole.

Publication Manual of the American Psychological Association. Fifth edition (2001). Washington, DC: American Psychological Association.

Richardson, J. T. E. (ed.) (1996). *Handbook of Qualitative Research Methods for Psychology and the Social Sciences*. Leicester: BPS Books.

Sommer, R. & Sommer, B. (2002). *A Practical Guide to Behavioral Research: Tools and Techniques*. Fifth edition. New York: Oxford University Press.

Wood, L. A. & Kroger, R. O. (2000). *Doing Discourse Analysis: Methods for Studying Action in Talk and Text*. Thousand Oaks, CA: Sage.

INDEX